CAMPAIGN 335

MORTAIN 1944

Hitler's Normandy Panzer offensive

STEVEN J. ZALOGA

ILLUSTRATED BY STEVEN NOON
Series Editor Marcus Cowper

OSPREY PUBLISHING
Bloomsbury Publishing Plc

Kemp House, Chawley Park, Cumnor Hill, Oxford OX2 9PH, UK
29 Earlsfort Terrace, Dublin 2, Ireland
1385 Broadway, 5th Floor, New York, NY 10018, USA
Email: info@ospreypublishing.com
www.ospreypublishing.com

OSPREY is a trademark of Osprey Publishing Ltd

First published in Great Britain in 2019
Transferred to digital print in 2022

A catalog record for this book is available from the British Library

Print ISBN: 978 1 4728 3252 8 – ePub: 978 1 4728 3251 1
ePDF: 978 1 4728 3250 4 – XML: 978 1 4728 3257 3

Maps by www.bounford.com
3D BEVs by The Black Spot
Index by Alan Rutter
Typeset by PDQ Digital Media Solutions, Bungay, UK
Printed and bound in India by Replika Press Private Ltd.

24 25 26 27 28   10 9 8 7 6 5

The Woodland Trust
Osprey Publishing supports the Woodland Trust, the UK's leading
woodland conservation charity.

www.ospreypublishing.com
To find out more about our authors and books visit our website. Here you
will find extracts, author interviews, details of forthcoming events and the
option to sign-up for our newsletter.

AUTHOR'S NOTE

The author would especially like to thank Ian Michael Wood for his help on
this book regarding German Panzer units, and Mark Reardon for his helpful
review of the manuscript. The photographs in this book, unless otherwise
noted, are from official US sources, principally US Army Signal Corps
photos. They were found at several archives including the US National
Archives in College Park, MD, the Special Collections at the US Military
Academy at West Point, NY, the Military History Institute at the US Army War
College at Carlisle Barracks, PA, and the Patton Museum at Ft. Knox, KY.

For brevity, the traditional conventions have been used when referring to
military units. In the case of US units, 2/120th Infantry refers to the 2nd
Battalion, 120th Infantry Regiment. The US Army traditionally uses Arabic
numerals for divisions and smaller independent formations (8th Division,
743rd Tank Battalion); Roman numerals for corps (VII Corps), spelled
numbers for field armies (Third US Army). In the case of German units, 2./
GR 919 refers to the 2nd Company, Grenadier-Regiment 919; II./GR 919
indicates the 2nd Battalion of Grenadier-Regiment 919. German corps
often were designated with Roman numerals such as XLVII. Panzer Korps,
but the alternate version 47. Panzer Korps is used here for clarity. Field
armies were designated in the fashion 7. Armee, but sometimes
abbreviated in the fashion AOK 7; the former style is used here.

GLOSSARY

GC&CS	Government Code and Cypher School at Bletchley Park
GFM	*Generalfeldmarschall*: field marshal
GMC	Gun Motor Carriage, often a tank destroyer
GR	Grenadier Regiment
Heer	German army
Heeresgruppe	Army Group, formation of several field armies
KG	*Kampfgruppe*: Battle group
Luftflotte	Air fleet
MHI	Military History Institute, Army Historical Education Center, Carlisle Barracks, PA
NARA	National Archives and Records Administration, College Park, MD
OB West	Oberbefehlshaber West: High Command West (Kluge's HQ)
PaK	Panzerabwehr Kanone: Anti-tank gun
SHAEF	Supreme Headquarters, Allied Expeditionary Force (Eisenhower's HQ)
SP	Self-propelled
Ultra	Code for decrypted German signals intelligence reports
Wehrmacht	German armed forces

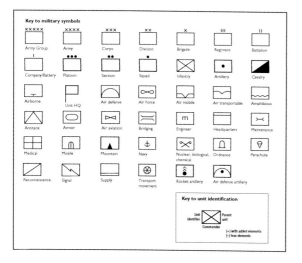

CONTENTS

Exploitation of the *Cobra* Breakthough, August 1–6, 1944

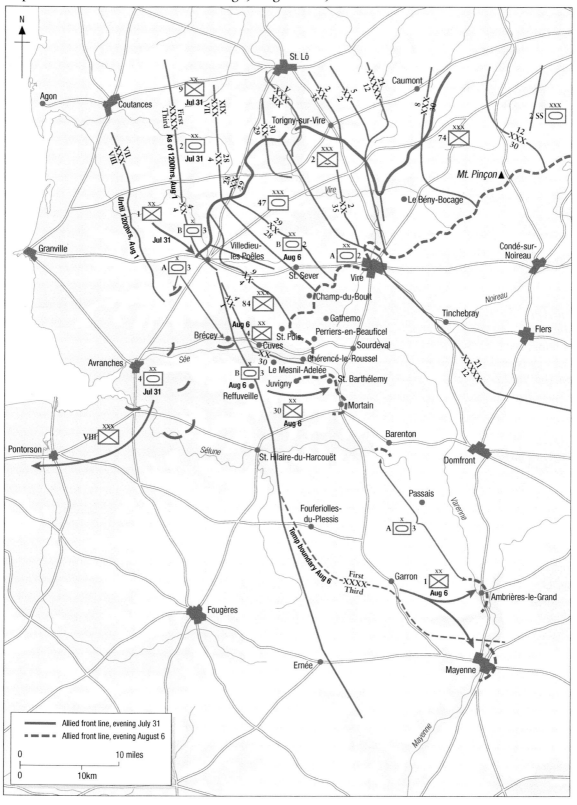

N

St. Lô

Agon

Coutances

Caumont

9 XX Jul 31

XIX XXX VII

V XXX XIX

XXXX 21 12

2 35

5 2

8 XXX 30

2 SS XXX

74 XXX

12 XXX 30

First XXXX Third As of 1200hrs, Aug 1

Torigny-sur-Vire

30 29

Vire

Mt. Pinçon ▲

2 XX Jul 31

28 XXX 4

2 XXX

Le Bény-Bocage

VII XXX VIII

1 XX Jul 31

27 28

4 4

4

47 XXX

29 XXX 28

B XX 2 Aug 6

A XX 2

Condé-sur-Noireau

Until 1200hrs, Aug 1

B X 3 Jul 31

Villedieu-les-Poêles

A X 3

9 4

St. Sever

Vire

Noireau

Granville

84 XXX

Champ-du-Boult

XX 4 Aug 6

Gathemo

Tinchebray

Flers

Brécey

Sée

St. Pois

Cuves

Perriers-en-Beauficel

Sourdeval

XX 30

Avranches

4 XX Jul 31

B X 3 Aug 6

Le Mesnil-Adelée

Chérencé-le-Roussel

XXXX 21 12

St. Barthélemy

Juvigny

Reffuveille

30 XX Aug 6

Mortain

VIII XXX

Pontorson

Sélune

St. Hilaire-du-Harcouët

Barenton

Domfront

Passais

Varenne

A X 3

Fouferiolles-du-Plessis

Temp boundary Aug 6

Fougères

First XXXX Third

Garron

1 XX Aug 6

Ambrières-le-Grand

Ernée

Mayenne

Mayenne

———— Allied front line, evening July 31

------- Allied front line, evening August 6

0   10 miles

0   10km

INTRODUCTION

On July 25, 1944, the First US Army launched its Operation *Cobra* offensive in Normandy.[1] Within a week, the offensive had succeeded in breaking through German defenses in Normandy. Hitler ordered a Panzer counter-attack, codenamed Operation *Lüttich* (*Liège*), to cut-off the American armored spearheads and to restore the German defensive perimeter in Normandy. The Panzer attack was aimed at re-capturing the port of Avranches, thereby sealing off the *Cobra* breakout. Operation *Lüttich* began in the early morning hours of August 6–7, 1944 but quickly stumbled into a costly stalemate. Hitler criticized the conduct of the attack and insisted that the offensive be revived using a larger and stronger force, the newly created Panzergruppe Eberbach. This had a profound effect on the German defense of Normandy, since it shifted the bulk of the Panzer forces away from the Caen sector where they had been resisting a

1   Steven Zaloga, *Operation Cobra 1944: Breakout from Normandy*, Osprey Campaign 88, 2001.

The advance of the 4th Armored Division into the port of Avranches on July 31, 1944 caused a crisis in the Wehrmacht in France. To avoid encirclement, Hitler ordered a Panzer offensive to recapture Avranches, which formed the basis for Operation *Lüttich*.

A column from the 28th Infantry, 8th Infantry Division march through Avranches on July 31, 1944 past an abandoned 8.8cm Flak gun. This division followed behind the 4th Armored Division into Brittany over the next week.

relentless series of British and Canadian tank offensives toward Falaise. Panzergruppe Eberbach never reached a critical mass sufficient to resist the onrush of the American 12th Army Group and the second phase of Operation *Lüttich* never took place. The misadventures of the Normandy Panzer force during the second week of August 1944 set the stage for the eventual entrapment and destruction of the German Army in Normandy in the Falaise pocket.

A column from the 2/18th Infantry, 1st Infantry Division advances through Juvigny-le-Tertre on August 3, passing by a burned-out M4 medium tank Task Force X, 3rd Armored Division knocked out the previous day. The 18th Infantry liberated Mortain later in the day.

CHRONOLOGY

July 20, 1944	Bomb plot against Hitler at the Wolf's Lair.
July 25	First US Army launches Operation *Cobra*.
July 30	Montgomery's 21st Army Group launches Operation *Bluecoat*.
August 1	12th Army Group activated under Gen. Omar Bradley.
1100hrs, August 1	Kluge suggests counter-attack to Avranches to the OKW.
2400hrs, August 2	Hitler approves Operation *Lüttich*.
August 3	1st Division liberates Mortain.
August 6	30th Division arrives in Mortain.
August 6	XV Corps, Third US Army begins advance eastward toward Le Mans.
1330hrs, August 6	Bletchley Park sends out an emergency Ultra signal about 47. Panzer-Korps attack.
2001hrs, August 6	Second emergency Ultra signal about Mortain attack.
2200hrs, August 6	Start of Operation *Lüttich*.
0100hrs, August 7	Bradley warns VII Corps about Mortain attack.
0038hrs, August 7	VII Corps warns 30th Division about Mortain attack.
1200hrs, August 7	2TAF begins air sorties against German columns in Mortain area.
1300hrs, August 7	Funck orders attacking forces to take up defensive positions to resist air attacks.
2200hrs, August 7	German attacks around Mortain resume under cover of darkness.
2200hrs, August 7	Canadian First Army launches Operation *Totalize* aimed at Falaise.
August 8	35th Division begins advance to the south of the Hilaire–Mortain road.
August 8	10. SS-Panzer-Division joins Lüttich offensive.
2000, August 8	Das Reich conducts spoiling attack on the 35th Division.
August 9	58. Panzer-Korps takes over southern wing Operation *Lüttich*.
August 8	Le Mans captured by XV Corps.

August 8	Bradley re-orients 12th Army Group offensive north toward Argentan.
August 10	XV Corps begins heading north toward Alençon.
August 10	VII Corps instructs the 35th Division to relieve Hill 314.
1300hrs, August 11	The 116. Panzer-Division begins movement toward Alençon.
2100hrs, August 11	German forces begin withdrawal from the Mortain area.
2400hrs, August 11	Hitler approves reorientation of Operation *Lüttich* to strike XV Corps.
0820hrs, August 12	320th Infantry, 35th Division reaches 2/120th Infantry on Hill 314.
August 12	XV Corps batters both 9. and 116. Panzer-Divisions around Alençon.
August 13	XV Corps starts, then halts, advance toward Argentan.
1200hrs, August 14	Canadian First Army launches Operation *Tractable* heading for Falaise.
August 15	Seventh US Army conducts Operation *Dragoon*, the amphibious invasion of southern France.
August 15	US armored divisions reach Chartres and Orleans, deep behind German lines.
1440hrs, August 15	Kluge issues preliminary orders for retreat from Normandy.
1700hrs, August 15	Hitler approves Kluge's retreat orders.
1900hrs, August 16	German troops authorized to begin retreat out of Normandy.
August 21	Argentan–Falaise Gap is closed.

THE OPPOSING COMMANDERS

GERMAN COMMANDERS

On July 20, 1944, a group of German army officers attempted a coup against Hitler at the "Wolf's Lair," his forward command post in East Prussia. He survived the bomb blast and the coup attempt quickly collapsed. The plot had a corrosive effect on subsequent German operations. Already distrustful of the German officer corps, the coup intensified Hitler's resentment. Hitler's micromanagement of German war efforts deprived German field commanders of vital tactical flexibility. Although Hitler made the final decisions on major operational matters, the key middleman between Hitler and the field commanders was **Generaloberst Alfred Jodl**, chief of operations of the OKW (Oberkommando der Wehrmacht: Armed Forces High Command) in Berlin.

Senior command of the Wehrmacht in France had changed significantly in July 1944. The western theater command, OB West (Oberbefehlshaber West), had been led by Generalfeldmarshall (GFM) Gerd von Rundstedt until July 2, 1944 when he was relieved by Hitler. **Günther Hans von Kluge** replaced Rundstedt. Kluge was one of Hitler's favorites, commander of 4. Armee during Germany's greatest feats of arms during the war, the envelopment of the French forces through the Ardennes in 1940. Kluge had a distinguished career on the Russian Front but was seriously injured in an automobile accident in October 1943. Kluge was a traditional Prussian officer who was nicknamed "Clever Hans" for his tendency toward political opportunism and vacillation. He was aware of earlier plots against Hitler

Generalfeldmarschall Günther Hans von Kluge, commander of OB West and Heeresgruppe B.

and was privy to the July 20 bomb plot. Suspicions about his loyalty were raised when the Gestapo interrogated one of his former aides. Kluge was anxious that his marginal role in the plot would result in his arrest. In fact, Hitler had told Alfred Jodl on August 1 that he knew that Rommel and Kluge were involved and that he would keep Kluge in place until the Avranches situation was cleaned up.

Generalfeldmarshall Erwin Rommel had led the anti-invasion front, Heeresgruppe B, in northern France and the Low Countries. He was seriously wounded on July 17, 1944 when a Spitfire strafed his staff car. In view of his complicity in the July 20 plot, he was offered the chance to commit suicide, which he did in October to save his family. Rommel had been an obstinate subordinate, so Kluge simplified the chain of command and took over control of Heeresgruppe B in late July 1944.

Heeresgruppe B had two principal commands in Normandy, 7. Armee in the western sector facing the Americans and Panzergruppe West in the east facing the British and Canadian forces near Caen. The 7. Armee was commanded by **Oberstgruppenführer Paul Hausser**, previous commander of II. SS-Panzer-Korps. He was a professional soldier who had earned the Iron Cross in World War I and retired from the Reichswehr in 1932 as a lieutenant-general. In the 1930s, he was involved in the formation of the early Waffen-SS formations, leading to his nickname "father of the Waffen-SS." By 1944, he was 64, 13 years older than his American counterpart, Omar Bradley.

Panzergruppe West had been led by **Leo Geyr von Schweppenburg** until July 2 when he was relieved of command after supporting Rundstedt's request for a retreat to a more defensible line in Normandy. He was replaced by **Generalleutnant Heinrich Eberbach**, an experienced tank commander. Eberbach served as the commander of Panzer-Regiment 35 of the 4. Panzer-

Division during the 1940 Battle of France, took over command of 4. Panzer-Division in 1942 and led 48. Panzer-Korps in November–December 1942 before being severely wounded during the fighting near Stalingrad. He served as Inspekteur der Panzertruppen des Heimatheeres (Inspector of the Homeland Panzer Troops) while recovering from his wounds.

The formation assigned to Operation *Lüttich* was 47. Panzer-Korps, led by **General der Panzertruppen Hans Freiherr von Funck**. He served in the Great War, and remained in the Reichswehr after the war, being appointed to the General Staff in 1933. He played a prominent role in German military activities in the Spanish Civil War in 1936–38. During the Battle of France in 1940, he led the 3. Panzer-Brigade. He took command of the 7. Panzer-Division in 1941, and was expected to head the Afrika Korps. However, he was distrusted by Hitler due to his pre-war connections to Werner von Fritsch, the army commander-in-chief relieved by Hitler in 1938. Regardless of Hitler's political suspicions, he was decorated with the Knight's Cross in July 1941, the German Cross in Gold on March 14, 1943 and the Knight's Cross with Oak Leaves on August 22, 1943, all while serving as commander of 7. Panzer-Division. Funck was appointed to the command of 47. Panzer-Korps on February 1, 1944. Hitler continued to have mixed feelings about Funck, and hours before the start of Operation *Lüttich*, he tried to have him replaced by Eberbach. However, it was too late to do so. Funck was relieved in early September and sent into the limbo of the army officer reserve.

General der Panzertruppen Hans Freiherr von Funck, commander of 47. Panzer-Korps

LEFT
General der Panzertruppen Gerhard Graf von Schwerin, commander of 116. Panzer-Division.

FAR LEFT
General der Panzertruppen Heinrich Freiherr von Lüttwitz, commander of 2. Panzer-Division during Operation *Lüttich*, and subsequently 47. Panzer-Korps after Funck was sacked.

There was a substantial reorganization of US Army commands on August 1 with the creation of the 12th Army Group under Lt. Gen. Omar Bradley (center). His former command, the First US Army, was handed over to Lt. Gen. Courtney Hodges (left) and Lt. Gen. George S. Patton (right) took command of the new Third US Army.

AMERICAN COMMANDERS

Lieutenant-General J. Lawton "Lighting Joe" Collins, commander of VII Corps.

The senior Allied commands were in a period of flux at the beginning of August 1944. Until then, overall command of Allied ground forces had been under the 21st Army Group, led by General Bernard L. Montgomery. The principal US command in Normandy had been First US Army under **Lt. Gen. Omar Bradley**. With the addition of **Lt. Gen. George Patton**'s Third US Army at the beginning of August, the two American field armies were subordinated to the new 12th Army Group under Bradley, with **Lt. Gen. Courtney Hodges** taking over First US Army command.

Bradley had been a classmate of Eisenhower's at the US Military Academy at West Point in the class of 1915. Like Eisenhower, he had not served in combat during World War I, though he had served in the Mexican border war in 1916–17. He had distinguished himself as an infantry officer in the inter-war army, and attracted the attention of George C. Marshall, while an instructor at the infantry school in the early 1930s, and again while working on the General Staff in 1938. After raising the 82nd Division, he served as deputy commander of II Corps under Lt. Gen. George S. Patton in North Africa in 1943. In Sicily, Bradley served as a corps commander, again under Patton's command. Bradley and Patton had known each other from the 1920s when they had both served in Hawaii. They were a complete contrast in style and temperament: Bradley, the son of a poor Missouri sodbuster, and Patton, from a wealthy family with a long military tradition. While Patton's star waned after Sicily, Bradley's rose. Patton's decline began with an incident on Sicily where he slapped some shell-shocked soldiers for cowardice. Eisenhower had found Patton to be impetuous and difficult to control during his command of Seventh Army on Sicily. Bradley, in contrast, had proven himself to be an able and competent corps commander, if not so bold as Patton. After Patton made further impolitic outbursts to the press in England, his career went into hibernation, making Bradley the choice to lead in France.

At the end of July 1944, the First US Army in Normandy had four corps of which the VII Corps played the central role in the Mortain fighting. The VII Corps had spearheaded the First US Army campaign to liberate Cherbourg in June 1944, and it also played the central role in the Operation *Cobra* break-out in late July. The VII Corps was led by **Maj. Gen. J. Lawton Collins**. He was one of the few senior US Army commanders to fight in both the Pacific and European theaters, the other being **Charles H. Corlett**, who commanded the XIX Corps on the left flank. Collins had commanded an infantry division during the fighting on Guadalcanal, where he picked up his nickname, "Lightning Joe," based on his radio call-sign. He was widely regarded as one of the most talented corps commanders in the European Theater of Operations (ETO) and would go on to become army chief-of-staff after the war.

BELOW LEFT
Lieutenant-General Wade Haislip, commander of XV Corps.

BELOW RIGHT
Major-General Leland Hobbs, commander of the 30th Infantry Division.

OPPOSING FORCES

GERMAN FORCES

The forces under OB West had suffered substantial casualties in the June–July 1944 Normandy campaign, with about 145,000 casualties including 17,100 dead and 72,000 missing. Casualties during the first week of August were a further 15,000. Replacements failed to keep pace with losses. Through mid-July, OB West received 27,125 replacements, but only 10,075 actually reached front-line units. The Normandy front survived by transfers of units from neighboring Brittany and the Pas-de-Calais. However, this cupboard was becoming bare by late July 1944. Continued transfers from Brittany and southern France substantially undermined subsequent campaigns in those areas, making prolonged defense there untenable.

The primary force allotted to Operation *Lüttich* was 47. Panzer-Korps. It was transferred from the Russian Front to France in the spring of 1944 and served under Heeresgruppe B during the Normandy campaign. Its component elements were primarily four Panzer divisions.

The German Panzer divisions of 1944 were significantly different in composition and strength to US armored divisions. The German divisions generally contained two tank battalions versus three in a US division, and six battalions of Panzergrenadiers versus three battalions of armored infantry. As a result, the US Armored Division had fewer personnel, 10,615 men versus 14,013. This was largely due to the defensive orientation of German operations since 1943, and the consequent need for a larger infantry component in such conditions. There were also some differences between the Heer (regular Army) and Waffen-SS divisions, with the Waffen SS Divisions having a somewhat more lavish table of organization and equipment as well as some components lacking in Heer divisions, such as multiple rocket artillery battalions.

A closer examination of the divisions participating in Operation *Lüttich* shows the significant gulf between the authorized strength of German Panzer divisions in 1944 and their actual strength. The three mechanized divisions available in in the 7. Armee sector were badly smashed from Operation *Cobra*. Panzer Lehr Division had been destroyed and took no part in Operation *Lüttich*. The 2. SS-Panzer-Division "Das Reich" had arrived in Normandy from southern France in June 1944 before Operation *Cobra*. The division lost most of its armored vehicles in the Roncey pocket during the *Cobra* battles but a substantial portion of its Panzergrenadier regiments had escaped. Tank strength after *Cobra* was only about two-dozen tanks and eight assault guns. To make up for casualties and the shortage of replacements, the Panzergrenadier regiments consolidated their organization to two instead of three battalions.

The 17. SS-Panzergrenadier-Division "Gotz von Berlichingen" was exhausted at the start of Operation *Cobra*, consisting of only two weak infantry battalions, five exhausted battalions and ten StuG IV assault guns. During the subsequent fighting against the *Cobra* breakout and the ensuing encirclement in the Roncey pocket, it was nearly destroyed. On August 4, 1944 its SS-Panzerjäger-Abt. 17 with 31 Jagdpanzer IVs reached northwestern France, but this battalion was committed to fighting around Laval and did not take part in the Mortain fighting with the rest of the division. The division's surviving combat forces were consolidated into battlegroups that were attached to Das Reich. These formations were grouped together as "Kampfgruppe 17" in Das Reich. Kampgruppe Fick, commanded by Ostubaf. Jakob Fick, contained most of the remnants of the Panzergrenadier units and numbered about 355 men including about 130 riflemen. Kampfgruppe Ullrich, consisting of the troops of the two Panzergrenadier heavy companies and assorted other units, totaled about 300 men.

The paucity of Panzer forces in 7. Armee meant that most of the units would have to come from Panzergruppe West. The 2. Panzer-Division had already been transferred to 7. Armee in late July in an attempt to rebuff the *Cobra* breakout. By early August, its strength had been reduced to about 60 tanks and its infantry strength significantly depleted; precise figures are lacking. The 116. Panzer-Division also had been transferred from

The 116. Panzer-Division was already heavily engaged in the sector along the Vire River in early August prior to Operation *Lüttich*. This Jagdpanzer IV of the division's Pz.Jg.Abt. 228 was knocked out by an M4 medium tank supporting the 4th Infantry Division during the fighting on August 2 northeast of Coulouvray-Boisbenâtre and is seen here being towed off the road.

The 9. Panzer-Division was shifted from southern France in early August with the intention of adding it to the Operation *Lüttich* force. In the event, the situation south of Mortain around Mayenne became so serious that it was diverted to take part in the defense there against the southern wing of VII Corps. This is an Sd.Kfz. 251 Ausf. D knocked out by a US tank destroyer on a road near Monsurs on August 9. The GI running by the wreck is armed with an M1 rifle fitted with a rifle grenade.

Panzergruppe West at the end of July in an attempt to stem *Cobra*. The 116. Panzer-Division had 77 tanks and AFVs on hand at the beginning of August.

Kluge was promised the 9. Panzer-Division from Heeresgruppe G in southern France, but it would take time to arrive. On August 6, it clashed with the 1st Infantry Division near Mayenne, and never took part in the *Lüttich* attack. Its Panther battalion was refitting and did not join the division until mid-August near Argentan, by which time the rest of the division had been shattered.

The 1. SS-Panzer-Division "Leibstandarte SS Adolf Hitler" (LSSAH) was the strongest formation of the attack force. At the time of the attack, it had 152 tanks and AFVs including 75 PzKpfw IVs (14 in repair); 54 Panthers (14 in repair) and 23 StuG III assault guns. It was at full strength in infantry. Due to the delays in reaching the Mortain area, only SS-Panzeraufklarungs-Abt. 1 and five tank companies from SS-Panzer-Regiment 1 arrived in time to take part in the initial attack. These were subordinated to 2. Panzer-Division. The remainder of the division did not arrive until the evening of Monday, August 7.

47. PANZER-KORPS	GEN. DER PANZERTRUPPEN HANS FREIHERR VON FUNCK
2. Panzer-Division	**Gen. der Panzertruppen Heinrich Freiherr von Lüttwitz**
Panzer-Regiment 3	
Panzergrenadier-Regiment 2	
Panzergrenadier-Regiment 304	
Panzer-Artillerie-Regiment 74	
Panzer-Aufklärungs-Abt. 2	
Panzerjäger-Abt. 38	
116. Panzer-Division	**Gen. der Panzertruppen Gerhard Graf von Schwerin**
II./Panzer-Regiment 16	
I./Panzer-Regiment 24	
Panzergrenadier-Regiment 60	
Panzergrenadier-Regiment 156	

The Panzer regiments in Panzer divisions in the summer of 1944 generally had a battalion of PzKpfw IV tanks and a battalion of the newer Panther tank. This is a PzKpfw IV Ausf. H of I./Pz.Rgt. 33 of the 9. Panzer-Division knocked out during the fighting around Sées in mid-August 1944.

Panzer-Artillerie-Regiment 146
Panzer-Aufklärungs-Abt. 116
Panzerjäger-Abt. 228

1. SS-Panzer-Division "LSSAH"   Brigadeführer Theodor Wisch
SS-Panzer-Regiment 1
SS-Panzergrenadier-Regiment 1
SS-Panzergrenadier-Regiment 2
SS-Panzer-Artillerie-Regiment 1
SS-Panzer-Aufklärungs.Abt. 1
SS-Sturmgeschütz-Abt. 1

2. SS-Panzer-Division "Das Reich"   Standartenführer Otto Baum
SS-Panzer-Regiment 2
SS-Panzergrenadier-Regiment 3 "Deutschland"
SS-Panzergrenadier-Regiment 4 "Der Führer"
Kampfgruppe 17 (17. SS-Pz.Gr.Div GvB)
SS-Panzer-Artillerie-Regiment 2
SS-Panzer-Aufklärungs-Abt. 2
SS-Sturmgeschütz-Abt. 2

The 116. Panzer-Division suffered moderate casualties in the fighting prior to *Lüttich* while trying the restrain the First US Army break-out. This is Panther number 351, the tank of Rittmeister von Günther, commander of Schwadron 3, I./Pz.Rgt. 24 knocked out during fighting with the 3rd Armored Division and 4th Infantry Division near Bas-Bois, between Saint-Pois et Coulouvray-Boisbenâtre, on August 3, 1944.

SS-Panzerjäger-Abteilung 17 fought separately from the rest of the division in August, taking part in the defense effort west of Le Mans against the US Army XV Corps. This is a Jagdpanzer IV from 2./SS-Pz. Jg.Abt. 17 knocked out on August 8 near Coulans-sur-Gée on the approaches to Le Mans during an encounter with the 90th Division, supported by the 712th Tank Battalion. Nine Jagdpanzers were knocked out in this fighting. This vehicle was photographed in early September 1944 when visited by a visiting delegation of US labor leaders.

In complete contrast to the Allied air forces, the Luftwaffe was never a significant factor in Normandy. The Luftwaffe fighter force had been shattered in the spring 1944 air campaigns while attempting to defend the Reich against American daylight bombing attacks. The Luftwaffe's Luftflotte 3 had three fighter groups in northwestern France in late July and had about 350 combat aircraft operational per day. They had a sortie rate of about 450 daylight missions and 250 night missions. In spite of this level of effort, only about 30 to 40 sorties per day actually reached their intended target area. Allied signals intelligence had cracked the Luftwaffe codes, and as a result, the Allied air forces had an unusually detailed glimpse at Luftwaffe plans and deployments. For example, on the Luftwaffe's busiest day, July 28, only 47 aircraft reached US lines of which 14 were shot down. A higher percentage of night sorties reached Allied lines, but these were ineffective due to poor bombing accuracy at night, and the presence of Allied night fighters.

US FORCES

Operation *Lüttich* struck the VII Corps and the initial blow was absorbed almost entirely by the 30th Infantry Division, nicknamed "Old Hickory." This division was originally formed in 1940 by federalizing the North Carolina, South Carolina, Georgia, and Tennessee National Guards. Like many of the National Guard divisions, it lost much of its National Guard flavor due to the replacement of many of its National Guard senior officers by Regular Army officers, as well as the churn in its enlisted personnel in the years from its formation to its combat debut in June 1944. The "Old Hickory" Division fought in the "Battle of the Hedgerows" near St. Lô in

The tank destroyer battalions attached to infantry divisions in Normandy were often equipped with the towed 3in. anti-tank gun. It proved to be too heavy and cumbersome, especially in view of its indifferent anti-armor performance. They were usually employed from static ambush positions, as was the case with this gun seen in France during the Operation *Lüttich* fighting.

June–July 1944. In 15 days of fighting around St. Lô, the 30th Division sustained 3,934 battle casualties, a loss rate of 25 percent for the unit as a whole but 90 percent in its rifle platoons, where three out of every four casualties occurred. The division was highly regarded and was widely considered one of the best US infantry divisions in the ETO.

30TH INFANTRY DIVISION	MAJ. GEN. LELAND HOBBS
117th Infantry Regiment	**Lt. Col. Walter M Johnson**
1st Battalion	Lt. Col. Robert Frankland
2nd Battalion	Lt. Col. James Lockett
3rd Battalion	Lt. Col. Samuel T. McDowell
119th Infantry Regiment	**Col. Edwin M Sutherland**
1st Battalion	Maj. Robert Herlong
2nd Battalion	Lt. Col. Edwin Wallis
3rd Battalion	Lt. Col. Courtney Brown
120th Infantry Regiment	**Col. Hammond Birks**
1st Battalion	Lt Col. William Bradford
2nd Battalion	Lt. Col. Hardaway
3rd Battalion	Lt. Col. Paul McCollum
Divisional Artillery	**Brig. Gen. James M Lewis**
113th Field Artillery Battalion (155mm)	
118th Field Artillery Battalion (105mm)	
197th Field Artillery Battalion (105mm)	
230th Field Artillery Battalion (105mm)	
105th Engineer Combat Battalion	
105th Medical Battalion	
30th Reconnaissance Troop (Mecz)	
Attachments	
743rd Tank Battalion	
823rd Tank Destroyer Battalion	

OPPOSING PLANS

GERMAN PLANS

Days before the start of Operation *Cobra*, OB West commander Kluge penned an assessment to Hitler in which he warned: "The moment is approaching when despite all efforts, the hard-pressed front will break. And when the enemy has erupted into open terrain, considering the inadequate mobility of our forces, orderly and effective conduct of the battle will hardly be possible."

Operation *Lüttich* was the first major Panzer offensive in Normandy, even though several other Panzer operations had been planned. Indeed, the Panzer force was central to German operational doctrine in France. The Allied use of amphibious operations in the Mediterranean theater in 1942–44 had presented a new challenge to the German art of war. Amphibious landings could occur at a wide range of locations, making it futile to reinforce every potential landing beach. As Frederick the Great had quipped "Who defends everything, defends nothing." As a result, the German tactical response to Allied amphibious landings was to refrain from excessive fortification of potential landing beaches, and instead to rely on a mobile Panzer counter-attack force to crush the landing. This was attempted at Gela on Sicily in July 1943, at Salerno in September 1943, and at Anzio in January–February 1944. All of these Panzer counter-attacks failed, though all came close to success.

When planning the defense of France in 1944, the creation of a large Panzer force to counter-attack an Allied landing became an essential element of German efforts. Panzergruppe West was a strategic Panzer reserve, directly under the command of Adolf Hitler and the OKW. Rather than spread the Panzer divisions evenly along the coast, they were concentrated well behind the coast so they could be shifted where ever the Allies landed, whether it be in the west in Brittany or Normandy, or in the east around the Pas-de-Calais or the Belgian coast.

This policy was not without its critics. Erwin Rommel, who had been appointed in the autumn of 1943 to head the anti-invasion front, was its primary antagonist. He argued that the concept of a Panzer counter-attack as the primary means to repel an Allied amphibious invasion had repeatedly failed. He argued that instead of massing the Panzer divisions away from potential landing sites, that it was imperative to place the Panzer divisions near the beaches so that any amphibious landing could be quickly crushed. If the Allies gained a toe-hold on the beaches, they could not be dislodged by subsequent Panzer attacks. Allied naval gunfire would crush any such attack, as was demonstrated at Sicily, Salerno, and Anzio. Rommel's arguments were vigorously contested by Gen. der Panzertruppe Leo Geyr von Schweppenburg, commander of Panzergruppe West. In the event, Hitler sided with Geyr and kept most of the Panzer force in strategic reserve. As a concession to Rommel, a few Panzer divisions were moved nearer the coast.

On D-Day, only the 21. Panzer-Division was near the landing sites. Lacking permission from Berlin, it launched a half-hearted attack toward Sword Beach that evaporated without consequence. As Rommel had predicted, it became nearly impossible to use Panzergruppe West to quickly crush the Allied landing sites. Movement from the Panzer staging areas was hampered by Allied demolition of the French railway system and interdiction of the French road network by Allied fighter-bombers. A shortage of first-class divisions in Normandy forced Berlin to haphazardly commit the Panzer divisions to plug gaps in the German defenses, especially in the Caen sector.

The first attempt to employ Panzergruppe West in its intended fashion as a concentrated counter-attack force was planned for late June 1944. By this time, the fresh II. SS-Panzer Korps was beginning to arrive in the beach-head area. The *Schwerpunkt* (focal point) of the attack was along the boundary between the First US Army and the British Second Army, roughly along the Drôme River. Several options were prepared by Rommel's Chef des Generalstabes Heeresgruppe B (Chief of the General Staff, Army Group B) and circulated to senior headquarters on June 22. The prospects for this Panzer offensive were questionable even under the most optimistic scenarios. The offensive never took place due to the friction of war. The Panzer divisions were late in arriving due to Allied air attacks on rail and road lines. Allied pressure on the frontline made it very difficult for Panzergruppe West to keep the Panzer divisions in reserve since the available German infantry divisions were too weak on their own to resist the persistent Allied offensives. The June 22 plan ultimately was abandoned when the British Second Army launched Operations *Martlet* and *Epsom* on June 25, forcing the commitments of most of these fresh Panzer divisions to defensive missions in the Caen sector.

The concept of using Panzergruppe West to stage a decisive counter-attack remained on Hitler's mind through the entire summer. It was revived again in mid-July. Rommel outlined a basic plan on July 15, involving seven Panzer divisions. Hitler issued instructions for a surprise Panzergruppe West night attack to take place on August 1, 1944 in the Caen sector.

In order to conduct the August 1 attack, it was necessary to substitute infantry divisions for Panzer divisions in the Panzergruppe West sector. This took considerable time since the infantry divisions had to be transferred from other sectors, mainly Brittany and the Pas-de-Calais. In the event, the combined blows of the American Operation *Cobra* breakout on July 25–31 and the British Operation *Bluecoat* attack on July 30 pre-empted the planned August 1 Panzer offensive. However, the mission of the Panzer reserve took another turn in early August 1944 when it was re-directed to crush the Operation *Cobra* break-out instead of being used in the Caen sector.

The threat of the Operation *Cobra* breakout was most acute at its western most point when it pushed down the coast past the port of Avranches on July 31, threatening to envelope Heeresgruppe B from the rear. At 1100hrs on August 1, Kluge suggested to the OKW in Berlin that the situation could be redeemed and "the breakthrough could be averted if other fronts were stripped to the utmost." The Avranches corridor was relatively narrow, and so a bold attack to the sea seemed an attractive opportunity.

Operation *Lüttich*: the plan, August 6, 1944

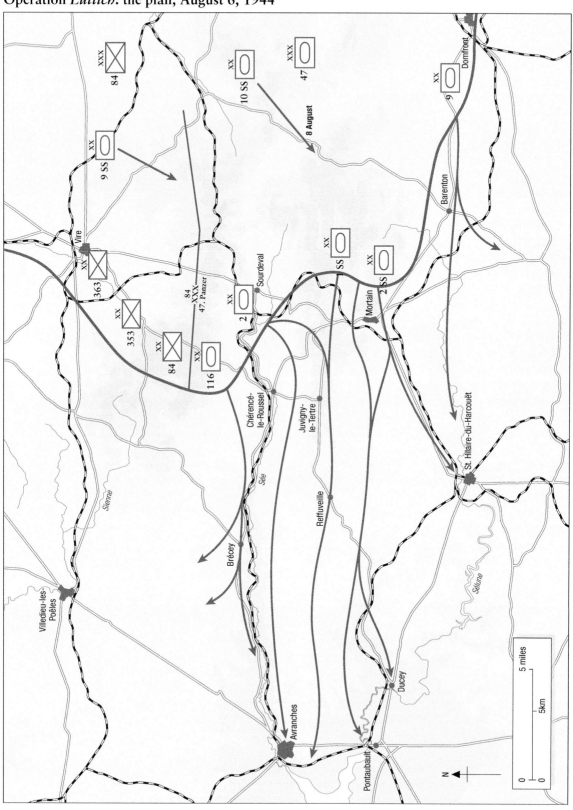

There were three possible avenues of advance to reach Avranches. The route north of the Sée River was ruled out immediately since it would be conducted through the bulk of the First US Army's strongest forces. The center routes from Mortain to Avranches between the Sée and Selune rivers offered good east–west roads, and for the moment at least, had very weak American forces. The main disadvantage was that the area's terrain was dominated by bocage, which Hausser judged to be "impossible for any large-scale employment of tanks." This factor was disregarded on the presumption that the attack would be conducted along the region's good roads without the need for a great deal of cross-country travel. The southern route through St. Hilaire-du-Harcouët had the advantage of being the furthest away from the advancing First US Army. However, Kluge and Hausser ruled it out since it was a far more elongated route than the others, and would have required time-consuming detours to reach the objectives. As a result, this option was also rejected in favor of the center route through Mortain.

Although Kluge had hoped to use two or more Panzer corps from Panzergruppe West for the attack, he was realistic enough to realize that such a large force could not be extracted quickly from the Caen front. Since he viewed time to be of the essence, he planned a more modest force with 47. Panzer-Korps as the main strike force, consisting of 2. Panzer-Division, 2. SS-Panzer-Division, and 116. Panzer-Division, with three infantry divisions to follow up to retain control of Avranches once it was retaken. Hausser complained that the Panzer divisions were too weak after recent combat to which Kluge retorted that they were still rated at Kampfwert 1 (Combat Value 1), meaning fully suitable for offensive missions. From surviving records, it would appear that detailed information on the strength of the Panzer divisions was lacking and out of date and the divisions much weaker than Kluge thought.

The counter-attack was codenamed Operation *Lüttich* (*Liège*), though many internal 7. Armee reports referred to it as Operation *Avranches*. Hitler formally approved Operation *Lüttich* in a directive to OB West around midnight on August 2–3. Hitler was unusually diffident about the plans for the counter-attack, still suffering from the after-effects of the bomb blast less than two weeks before. When asked by Jodl what should be done to respond to the American breakthrough, he told Jodl he "could publish orders to his heart's content. They would avail nothing. The time was too short." Hitler appeared to be pushing responsibility on to Kluge.

Kluge attempted to gather additional forces for the mission. The most obvious source of Panzer divisions was Panzergruppe West, which had been attempting to pull back units for the past two weeks for the stillborn August 1 Panzer offensive against the British. This offensive had been cancelled due to the relentless British attacks. The most recent of which, Operation *Bluecoat* on July 30, had forced the return of the Panzer divisions of II. SS-Panzer-Korps to the front. For the moment, I. SS-Panzer-Korps south of Caen seemed to be idle. On the morning of August 3, in a telephone conversation with OKW, Kluge attempted to get permission from Hitler to secure a Panzer division from I. SS-Panzer-Korps for the Avranches attack. Shortly after this conversation, Kluge was able to convince Eberbach to transfer the 1. SS-Panzer-Division to 47. Panzer Korps for the Avranches counter-attack. Jodl provided the final blessing from Berlin for this reinforcement in a telephone conversation with Kluge around noon on August 3.

At this point, Kluge thought he had Hitler's blessing to conduct *Lüttich* at his own discretion without further need to obtain permission for timing and other details from Berlin. Kluge was under the impression that Hitler wanted

An aerial view of Mortain taken after the war. Hill 314 can be seen to the right and Hill 285 to the left. The L'Abbaye Blanche monastery was located in the upper left slightly outside this image.

the attack conducted as soon as possible. Hitler appears to have become distant and distracted from the operation due to the trauma of his bomb injuries and unfolding disasters on many fronts, including the Warsaw uprising and the growing threat of the loss of Romania and its essential oil fields. He made little effort to micro-manage *Lüttich* for a few days after giving his original approval on August 3.

With the attack force shaping up, Kluge turned his attention to other necessary preparations for Operation *Lüttich*. In a telephone conversation with Hausser on the afternoon of August 3, Kluge outlined a realignment of the 7. Armee divisions in contact with the Americans northeast of Avranches. The timing of the offensive was largely dictated by the arrival of fresh infantry divisions to replace Panzer divisions assigned to the attack. The 2. Panzer-Division assembled southwest of Saint-Manvieu on the morning of August 4; the 2. SS-Panzer-Division southwest of Vire on August 5; and the 116. Panzer-Division on August 6. The most complicated transfer was the 1. SS-Panzer-Division, which began to be relieved on the night of August 4–5 by the 89. Infanterie-Division. Due to concern over Allied air power, the division moved westward only at night. While the 40–50 mile (70–80km) march route did not seem so difficult on paper, the actual transfer proved more time consuming than expected because II. SS-Panzer-Korps was being shifted to the left (western) wing of Panzergruppe West on the same nights along the same route to deal with a potential British breakthrough near Caumont.

Records for the overall armored vehicle strength of the 47. Panzer-Korps have not survived. From the scattered records that remain, it would appear that there were about 250 tanks and 60 assault guns/tank destroyers in 47. Panzer-Korps at the start of Operation *Lüttich*. This does not include the 9. Panzer-Division, which did not take part in this attack. By way of comparison, the US VII Corps had about 695 M4 medium tanks and 380 M5A1 light tanks operational on August 7, 1944; strength figures on M10 tank destroyers are lacking.

Adding to the turmoil before the attack, there was a flare-up between the commander of 116. Panzer-Division and the 47. Panzer-Korps commander. General Schwerin of the 116. Panzer-Division already had a string of arguments in late July about corps commander Funck's brusque and sarcastic command style. Funck had accused the 116. Panzer-Division of having "mucked it up" in the previous fighting on the Vire front and Schwerin expressed his reservations about the hasty planning for the Avranches offensive and the lack of even basic reconnaissance or intelligence gathering about opposing forces. On the afternoon of August 6, Lüttwitz reported to Funck that the promised Panther battalion from Schwerin had not arrived as promised in support of the 2. Panzer-Division. In fact, it had arrived, but this had not been reported in a timely fashion. Funck took this to be another example of Schwerin's insubordination and at 2200hrs on the evening of August 6, he asked Hausser to relieve Schwerin. Hausser balked at the demand, four hours before the start of the offensive.

The threat of Allied air attack was considered such a hazard that the attack was scheduled for nightfall at 2200hrs on Sunday, August 6. The intention was to conduct the initial penetration of the American defenses before dawn and the potential arrival of Allied fighter bombers. For surprise, there was no preparatory artillery bombardment.

Further complicating the prospects for *Lüttich*, the First US Army had pushed into the original *Lüttich* staging areas. The 1st Infantry Division had advanced into the northern portion of assembly area on August 2–3, capturing the road junction at Juvigny-le-Tertre and liberating Mortain on August 3. German forces in this area were mostly the skeletal remnants of infantry divisions smashed during Operation *Cobra*. One of the few bright spots was that the 84. Armee-Korps had still managed to hold the cross-roads town of Vire.

As if Kluge did not have enough problems in conducting Operation *Lüttich*, on the afternoon of August 6, Hitler refocused his attention back to the situation in Normandy. By this stage, Hitler had come under the medical attention of a Luftwaffe physician, Dr. Erwin Giesing. He began administering daily doses of cocaine, in addition to the drug cocktail already being administered by Hitler's primary physician, Theodor Morell. Hitler regained his confidence, and the old megalomania returned in force. He began micromanaging the field armies again.

On Sunday afternoon, August 6, hours before the start of the Avranches offensive, Hitler told Jodl to get details of the *Lüttich* plan by evening, not even realizing the attack was planned to start later that night. Interrupting his daily conference, Hitler also authorized the allotment of 60 Panther tanks recently delivered to the training grounds at Mailly-le-Camp to be available for Operation *Lüttich*. He also authorized the transfer of all PzKpfw IV tanks and armored cars of the 11. Panzer-Division in southern France to the Avranches strike force. These allotments were entirely fanciful since it would take days to move them to the Mortain area. After Hitler's conference ended, he made clear his opposition to Funck leading the Avranches attack and that he wanted the Panzergruppe West commander Eberbach instead. Hitler had expected that the operation would involve far more substantial forces and include several Panzer corps, not a single corps. Kluge responded that time was of the essence. Acknowledging Kluge's argument that it would take several additional days to amass such a force, Hitler then questioned whether it would be better to delay the Avranches attack. After discussions with Jodl and several other senior OKW planners, Hitler relented and allowed the attack to proceed, informing Kluge only a few hours before the planned start time of 2200hrs on the night of August 6.

Hitler still wanted a far grander attack than the one planned by Kluge. After re-capturing Avranches, he wanted the attack force to turn to the northwest to strike the flank of the First US Army. Hitler still had doubts over the loyalty of Kluge and Funck and he sent Gen. der Inf. Walter Buhle, chief of the army staff of the OKW, to Normandy by plane to watch over the operation. Buhle had been wounded during the July assassination attempt at the Wolf's Lair and he was viewed by Hitler as a bona-fide loyalist.

AMERICAN PLANS

At the start of August, Collins' VII Corps was part of the First US Army advance southeastward. In order to free up the coastal corridor for Patton's Third US Army to pass into Brittany, Collins' VII Corps began moving to the east, with the 3rd Armored Division providing the spearhead of the exploitation and the infantry divisions following behind and mopping up the German defenses. German defenses at Vire and Sourdeval proved to be far more tenacious than defenses further south near Mortain. The 1st Infantry Division passed through Juvigny-le-Tertre on August 2, and Mortain was liberated by the 18th Infantry, 1st Division on August 3. The 18th Infantry dug in around the town and repulsed a German counter-attack on August 4. The most prominent geographic feature of Mortain was Hill 314 to the east of the town. This provided a commanding view over most of the neighboring terrain and so was an obvious defensive position. The 18th Infantry dug in on Hill 314.

The 1st Division did not remain in the Mortain area very long. By this time, XV Corps from Patton's Third US Army was operating further south and turning eastward, with Le Mans as its immediate objective. In order to provide flank protection for this advance, the 1st Division was ordered further south toward Mayenne. Curiously enough, the 1st Division indirectly assisted in disrupting Operation *Lüttich* when it began to engage the 9. Panzer-Division near Mayenne on August 6 during its attempt to move into the *Lüttich* staging area.

After two weeks of intense fighting, several VII Corps divisions halted for rest and refurbishment, three of these to the west of Mortain. This included the 9th Infantry Division to the northwest of Mortain, and the 4th Infantry Division and 3rd Armored Division to the northwest.

The 30th Division was instructed to take over the 1st Division positions in and around Mortain. The 30th Division began arriving in the Mortain area on August 6, less than a day before the start of Operation *Lüttich*. The 30th Division deployed in the usual fashion, with two regiments forward and one regiment in reserve. The 117th Infantry was deployed in the vicinity of St. Barthélemy with 1/117th Infantry in the town itself, and the other two battalions behind the town on neighboring hills. The 120th Infantry was deployed in and around Mortain with two companies of 2/120th Infantry on Hill 314 east of town, and 1/120th Infantry on Hill 285 behind the town to the west. The 120th Infantry was able to use trenches dug by the 18th Infantry the previous few days. The 119th Infantry was in reserve to the northwest of Juvigny-le-Tertre.

INTELLIGENCE WARNINGS

VII Corps had picked up signs of the withdrawal of the 2. Panzer-Division and 116. Panzer-Division out of the front lines in the Vire sector in the early days of August, but the presumption was that this realignment was undertaken to avoid having these divisions caught in a trap.

In the early morning hours of August 2–3, the Government Code and Cypher School (GC&CS) at Bletchley Park in England received an intercepted communication from Hitler via the OKW to OB West and Heeresgruppe B stating that "The Panzer divisions which have up to now been employed on that [Caen] front must be released and transferred to the left wing. The enemy's tank forces which have pressed forward to the east, south-east and south will be annihilated by an attack which these Panzer divisions, numbering at least four, will make, and contact will be restored with the west coast of Contentin at Avranches, or north of that, without regards to the enemy penetrations into Brittany." This laid out the basic Operation *Lüttich* plan, though Allied intelligence did not yet know the date. On August 6, on the eve of the German attack, GC&CS began decrypting a flurry of radio communications that revealed the German attack plans hours before its start.

Most German army units used telephone, teletype or couriers for messages, which could not be intercepted by Allied signals intelligence. However, most of the Panzer divisions had a Luftwaffe Flivo (Fliegerverbindungsoffizier: Air Liaison Officer) attached. These officers usually communicated with higher headquarters via radio, with the messages encrypted by Enigma machines. The radio communications intercepted on Sunday, August 6, were mostly requests for Luftwaffe air cover for Operation *Lüttich*. The first message intercepted on August 6 was a II. Jagdkorps response to an army request for a "fighter operation in a strength of not less than 1,000 aircraft in a limited area" which II. Jagdkorps declared to be impossible. This message did not indicate the location, but clearly indicated a major operation was afoot.

At 1330hrs, Sunday August 6, Bletchley Park sent out an emergency signal to Ultra decrypt recipients in the ETO that the four Panzer divisions under 47. Panzer-Korps were planning an attack westward. At 1400hrs, the Flivo attached to 2. SS-Panzer-Division passed on a request for immediate night fighter cover over its staging area near St. Clement through to its immediate objective of St. Hillaire, and for daylight cover the following day. A second emergency Ultra signal was sent at 2001hrs on August 6 warning that 2. SS-Panzer Division would attack Mortain and then move on to St. Hilaire. A third Ultra emergency signal was issued at 0011hrs on the morning of August 7 that indicated that a II. Jagdkorps message had revealed that a Panzer attack by 7. Armee would begin on the evening of August 6 using five Panzer divisions with the Brécy-Montigny road as the first objective.

These warnings did not come as a complete surprise to senior US commanders. Bradley, Hodges, and Collins had already discussed the likelihood of a German counter-attack against the narrow Avranches corridor. Furthermore, First US Army G-2 (intelligence) had been tracking the transfer of divisions from the Caen sector westward. However, prior to the Ultra warning, there was no detail as to where or when the attack would take place. At 0010hrs, based on the initial Ultra warnings, First US Army HQ warned Collins at VII Corps, without revealing the source of the information, that the Germans were preparing a counterattack in his sector. Collins' VII Corps headquarters in turn passed this on to subordinate divisions, and at 0038hrs, the 30th Division received the warning of an attack toward Mortain "sometime in the next 12 hours." Collins instructed Hobbs to halt movement of the 119th Infantry until morning; to move a rifle battalion to Le Teileul, south of Mortain; and to reinforce the defenses on Hill 314. At the tactical level, the warnings came too late to have much impact. The 120th Infantry had already been under attack for about 90 minutes when its warning arrived.

While the Ultra warning messages had little immediate impact at the small-unit level, they had important consequences later on Monday, August 7. Knowledge of the scope of the German attack prompted senior US Army commanders to reinforce the Mortain sector, allot further artillery ammunition to the sector, and devote the First US Army's 32nd Field Artillery Brigade to repulsing the counter-attack. Patton's Third US Army was warned since its XX Corps was passing down the Avranches corridor at this time. On being informed of the Ultra warnings, Patton ordered the 35th Division, 80th Division, and French 2e Division Blindée to halt in the St. Hillaire area in the event their re-deployment was necessary. These forces would have constituted a counter-attack force had the Germans actually broken through.

In addition, the USAAF's IX and XIX Tactical Air Commands and the RAF's 2nd Tactical Air Force were warned of the attack. At 2300hrs, Brig. Gen. Otto Weyland of XIX Tactical Air Command telephoned Lt. Gen. Elwood "Pete" Quesada of IX Tactical Air Command to discuss their combined response to the threat since the German attack area was near the border of their respective commands. XIX Tactical Air Command had only recently become operational to support Patton's Third US Army, and it was allotted the primary responsibility for the USAAF air operations over Mortain. Quesada offered to subordinate any necessary air units to Weyland's command, but Weyland limited his request to the 406th Group, equipped with rocket-armed P-47 Thunderbolts, as well as some P-51 Mustang squadrons for top cover.

At the senior level, Maj. Gen. Hoyt S. Vandenberg, commander of the USAAF 9th Army Air Force, spoke with Air Marshal Sir Arthur Coningham, commander of the RAF's 2nd Tactical Air Force, reaching an agreement under which the RAF's rocket-armed Hawker Typhoons would take on the primary responsibility for tank-busting while US fighters would provide air cover against the Luftwaffe and attack German motor transport. Coningham, an ardent advocate of close-air support, saw this as an opportunity to prove the value of tactical air power. In turn, the tactical details were left to Quesada and Air Vice Marshal Harry Broadhurst, commander of the RAF's 83 Group, 2nd Tactical Air Force. The coordination of the Allied air forces on August 6–7, initiated by the Ultra revelations, would play a vital role in the defeat of Operation *Lüttich*.

While it did not have an immediate impact on the initial Mortain fighting, important changes in Allied plans regarding the direction of Patton's Third US Army would further undermine Operation *Lüttich*. In the wake of the capture of Avranches, Bradley's 12th Army Group became bifurcated with Hodges' First US Army heading east toward the Seine while Patton's Third US Army veered west into Brittany. The decision to advance into Brittany to seize the major ports was a central element of the original *Overlord* plans since it was presumed they would be essential to keep Allied forces supplied for the autumn campaign.[2] This plan was blindly followed at the end of July. By the first week of August, doubts began to emerge. It was becoming increasingly clear that German defenses in Normandy were collapsing. Rather than waste Patton's Third US Army in Brittany, it could accelerate the destruction of Heeresgruppe B in Normandy by moving east toward Le Mans instead of west toward Brest. Major-General John Wood, a pioneer of the US armored force and commander of the 4th Armored Division, was the first to make this suggestion, immediately convincing Patton of its merits. In turn, Patton convinced Bradley, and Bradley convinced Montgomery and Eisenhower. On August 8, a day after the start of Operation *Lüttich*, Patton was authorized to reorient his forces eastward, leaving only a corps in Brittany. This would have trapped the attacking 47. Panzer Corps between First US Army and Third US Army had *Lüttich* in fact approached Avranches.

2   Steven Zaloga, *Brittany 1944: Hitler's Last Defenses in France*, Osprey Campaign 320, 2018.

THE CAMPAIGN

The start of Operation *Lüttich* was a shambles. The attack was first scheduled to start after sunset at 2200hrs, on the night of August 6–7. At 2200hrs, Funck telephoned Hausser telling him that many of the columns were behind schedule and recommending that the attack be postponed. He complained that the main elements of 1. SS-Panzer-Division were still six miles (10km) from the start line, and that, so far, only its reconnaissance battalion and a company of PzKpfw IV tanks had arrived. Hausser dismissed the idea of a delay as "utter madness" and told Funck to get on with the attack. To further complicate matters, the late-arriving Panzer companies of 1. SS-Panzer-Division shared some of the same roads as those assigned to 2. SS-Panzer-Division, leading to a traffic jam that delayed the start of some "Das Reich" units.

Due to the warm summer weather and high humidity, ground fog was common in the early morning hours. This was welcomed by the attacking German forces since it promised to offer cover from Allied air attack so long as it lasted.

THE DAS REICH ATTACK

The principal attack on Mortain was conducted by 2. SS-Panzer-Division "Das Reich." Prior to the attack, its staging area was around near St. Martin-de-Chaulieu, about ten miles (16km) from Mortain. The division attacked in three groups.

Mortain is located in a shallow valley with Hill 314 to the east and Hill 285 to the northwest. This is a view of the town from the southwest around Les Fresnaies with Hill 314 in the background.

Operation *Lüttich*, August 7, 1944

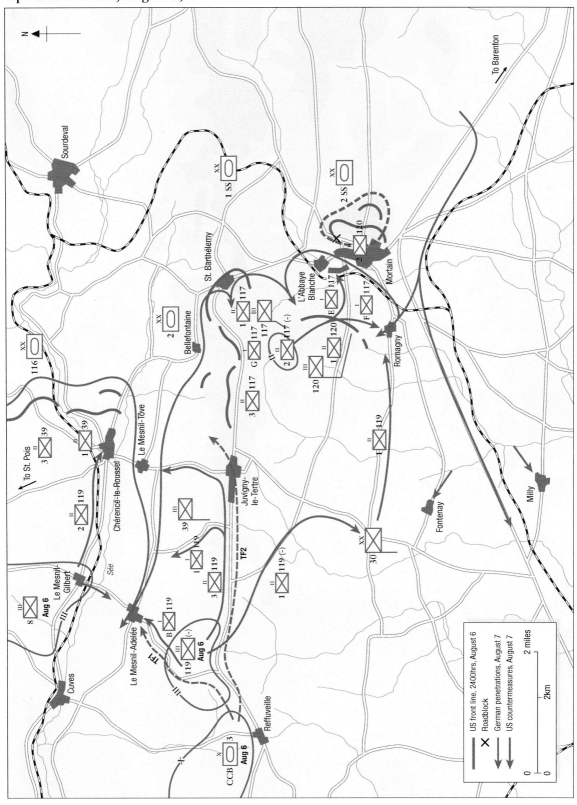

The principal column was based around Gunther Wisliceny's SS-Panzergrenadier-Regiment 3 "Deutschland" with the understrength SS-Panzer-Regiment 2 in support. Their mission was to secure the town of Mortain itself as well as the surrounding hills. Attached to this formation was Kampfgruppe 17, the remnants of 17. SS-Panzergrenadier Division, supported by a company of the Das Reich's StuG III assault guns.

The northern Das Reich attack force was Otto Weidinger's SS-Panzergrenadier-Regiment 4 "Der Führer" supported by the other company of StuG III assault guns. This attacked in a column with the III./SS-Pz.Gren.Rgt. 4 followed by II./SS-Pz.Gren.Rgt. 4. This formation attacked to the north of Mortain with the L'Abbaye Blanche monastery as their immediate objective.

The smallest formation was Ernst Krag's SS-Panzeraufklärungs-Regiment 2, which was assigned the usual reconnaissance/cavalry role as flank guard, covering the division to the south by establishing blocking positions in Bion and St. Jean-de-Corail.

The town of Mortain was defended by two battalions from the 120th Infantry, 30th Division with the 3/120th Infantry having been posted further south at Barenton. Colonel Hammond Birks, the regimental commander, believed that the main threat came from the northeast and so oriented the defenses most strongly in that direction. Most of the 1/120th Infantry was located on Hill 285 to the northwest of town, and the 2/120th Infantry along with Co. K, 3/120th Infantry, on Hill 314. The town itself was used mainly for headquarters and support units with roadblocks established on the main north–south roads leading into town.

In spite of the scheduled time of 2200hrs for the attack, fighting began spasmodically due to the traffic problems and inevitable difficulties of conducting road marches at night. Kampfgruppe 17 arrived in the Mortain

The initial attacks on Monday morning, August 7 were conducted in heavy ground fog. This is a pair of Panther Ausf. A tanks of 3./SS-Pz. Rgt. 1 knocked out in the fighting to the northwest of St. Barthélemy.

EVENTS

1. Kampfgruppe Fick attack Co. G/120th Infantry position but takes heavy losses in the process.

2. Kampfgruppe Fick also attacks Co. H, the 2/120th Infantry's heavy weapons company, and overruns and disperses it.

3. Company E, 120th Infantry attacked by elements of Kampfgruppe 17 supported by Das Reich StuG III assault guns.

4. At 0235hrs, Col. Birks, the 120th Infantry commander orders his reserve company, C/1/120th Infantry, to move to Hill 314.

5. Kampfgruppe Ullrich infiltrates past the northern side of Mortain, then overruns small roadblocks of 1/120th Infantry near the base of Hill 285. The main attack is supported by a company of four Das Reich StuG III assault guns. The attacks are eventually stopped and the armored support stripped away with bazooka fire and 3in. anti-tank guns from the 823rd Tank Destroyer Battalion attached to the 1/120th Infantry.

6. Wisliceny's battlegroup splits into two columns with I./SS-Pz.Gren.Rgt. 3 heading directly into Mortain, II./SS-Pz.Gren.Rgt. 3 goes westward toward the village of Romagny along with some of the tanks of SS-Pz.Rgt. 2.

7. A battlegroup of SS-Pz.Rgt. 2 heads down the road to St. Hillaire-du-Harcouët.

8. I./SS-Pz.Gren.Rgt. 3 penetrates the southern outpost line of Mortain starting around 0130hrs. The Panzergrenadiers overrun the 3rd Platoon, Co. A, 823rd Tank Destroyer Battalion and outposts of Co. F, 120th Infantry.

9. Before Co. C, 120th Infantry reaches Hill 314, it is diverted from its original mission, with two of its platoons remaining in Mortain to defend the town. They are unable to establish a coherent defense and I./SS-Pz.Gren.Rgt. 3 gains full control of Mortain by 1000hrs.

10. Lead elements of Wisliceny's II./SS-Pz.Gren.Rgt. 3 reach Romagny and are temporarily halted by the Intelligence and Reconnaissance Platoon of the 120th Infantry.

11. Around 0500hrs, the spearhead of SS-Pz.Gren.Rgt. 4 "Der Führer", a column led by 9. Kompanie, III./SS-Pz.Rgt. 4 runs into the l'Abbaye Blanche roadblock based on Lt. Tom Springfield's 1st Platoon, Company A, 823rd Tank Destroyer Battalion, reinforced by 57mm anti-tank guns of the AT Company, 120th Infantry embedded in an infantry strongpoint led by Lt. Tom Andrew of 1st Platoon, Co. F, 120th Infantry. In the ensuing firefight, six Sd.Kfz. 251 armored half-tracks and several other vehicles are left burning and the attack halted.

12. Around dawn, Lt. Col. J.W. Lockett's 2nd Battalion, 117th Infantry, minus Co. G, attempts to re-establish control of Mortain itself, supported by eight M4 tanks of the 743rd Tank Battalion. The bulk of the battalion under Lt. Col. Lockett along with four tanks heads into town but are unable to breach German defenses. Company F with four tanks moves down the road on the western side of town to reach Romagny but are unable to do so, though they do manage to keep the road open near Neufbourg.

13. Later in the day, Lockett deploys Co. E, 117th Infantry to reinforce the L'Abbaye Blanche roadblock.

DAS REICH ATTACK ON MORTAIN, AUGUST 7, 1944

WEIDINGER

AMERICAN UNITS
30th Division
1/120th Infantry
A. Co. A, 120th Infantry
B. Co. B, 120th Infantry
C. Co. C, 120th Infantry
2/120th Infantry
D. Co. E, 2/120th Infantry
E. Co. F, 2/120th Infantry
F. Co. G, 2/120th Infantry
G. Co. H, 2/120th Infantry
H. Co. K, 3/120th Infantry
I. I&R Platoon, 120th Infantry
Abbaye Blanche Roadblock
J. 1st Platoon, Company A, 823rd Tank Destroyer Battalion (four 3in. AT guns)
K. AT Company, 120th Infantry (four 57mm AT guns)
117th Infantry (-)
L. Co. E, 2nd Battalion, 117th Infantry
M. Co. F, 2nd Battalion, 117th Infantry

WISLICENY

Note: Gridlines are shown at intervals of 1km (0.6 miles)

This is a view looking up the road from Mortain toward L'Abbaye Blanche as would have been seen by Das Reich units attacking the American roadblock further up the road toward the upper left. The monastery was located beyond the buildings in the center.

area before Wisliceny's columns from SS-Pz.Gren.Rgt. 3, and began infiltrating into the woods around the base of Hill 314 around midnight. One of its two battlegroups, Kampfgruppe Fick, hit the Co. G/120th Infantry position but took heavy losses in the process. The neighboring Co. H, the 2/120th Infantry's heavy weapons company, was not positioned for close combat and its mortar platoon was overrun. Company E, 120th Infantry was on the southernmost crest of Hill 314. Its positions were hit by elements of Kampfgruppe 17 supported by Das Reich StuG III assault guns. By 0235hrs, it was clear that the 2/120th Infantry was in trouble on Hill 314. Colonel Birks ordered his reserve company, C/1/120th Infantry, to move to Hill 314 to reinforce the embattled 2nd Battalion.

While Kampfgruppe Fick was entangled with elements of the 2/120th Infantry on the central and southern portions of Hill 314, Kampfgruppe Ullrich from Kampfgruppe 17 managed to infiltrate past the northern side of Mortain toward its objective, Hill 285. This position was held by two companies of the 1/120th Infantry. Kampfgruppe Ullrich overran small roadblocks near the base of the hill and then began attacking the Co. A and Co. B positions with the aid of a StuG III assault gun until the Co. B commander, Lt. Pulver, used a bazooka to knock it out. Close-range fighting continued through dawn. When the fog finally lifted by mid-morning, Kampfgruppe Ullrich made another attempt to overcome the 1/120th Infantry defenses on Hill 285, but two of the accompanying StuG III assault guns from Das Reich were knocked out by towed 3in. anti-tank guns from the 823rd Tank Destroyer Battalion that were attached to the battalion.

The southern wing of the attack bumped into outposts of the 4th Cavalry well south of Mortain in the dark. The approach route of Wisliceny's SS-Pz. Gren.Rgt. 3 was toward Mortain from the south, and the columns arrived in the villages of Bion and St. Jean-du-Corail shortly after midnight. Krag's reconnaissance battalion stayed behind in these villages as flank security. At

One of the 3in. M5 anti-tank guns of the 823rd Tank Destroyer Battalion knocked out during the fighting around Mortain. The right splinter shield of the gun has been blown off.

this point, Wisliceny's battlegroup split into two columns with I./SS-Pz.Gren. Rgt. 3 heading directly into Mortain, and II./SS-Pz.Gren.Rgt. 3 along with some of the tanks of SS-Panzer-Regt. 2 going westward along the Mortain-Hillaire road toward the village of Romagny to the southwest.

I./SS-Pz.Gren.Rgt. 3 reached the southern approaches of Mortain around 0130hrs. This group advanced into town on foot and was able to infiltrate through the thin American defenses. This area was much more weakly defended than the northern and eastern approaches to the town. The Panzergrenadiers overran the 3rd Platoon, Co. A, 823rd Tank Destroyer Battalion, which lacked any infantry screen. Outposts of Co. F, 120th Infantry were also hit in the dark.

Before Co. C, 120th Infantry reached Hill 314, it was diverted from its original mission, with two of its platoons remaining in Mortain to defend the town. Only the 3rd Platoon of Co. C reached the crest of Hill 314 where it was directed to reinforce Co. K on the northern side. The two platoons of Co. C assigned to defend the town were instructed to advance to the south side of town and set up new roadblocks. By this time, Wisliceny's Panzergrenadiers had thoroughly infiltrated the town and Co. C was never able to establish a coherent defense.

The Panzergrenadiers reached the hotel that housed the command post of 2/120th Infantry, but the headquarters

This is the view from the perspective of the southernmost portion of the American roadblock in L'Abbaye-Blanche looking southward toward Mortain from which Das Reich units would have approached. The same small shed can be seen in the center both of these photos.

DEFENSE OF THE ABBAYE BLANCHE ROADBLOCK, AUGUST 7, 1944 (PP. 36–37)

The northern portion of the 2. SS-Panzer-Division "Das Reich" attack against Mortain was delayed in the pre-dawn hours when its advancing columns became caught up in a traffic jam with 1. SS-Panzer-Division. As a result of this delay, Otto Weidinger, the commander of SS-Pz.Gren.Rgt. 4 "Der Führer," decided to conduct a mounted attack into Mortain lead by the 9. Kompanie. This Panzergrenadier company was part of the III. Bataillon (Gepanzerte), the regiment's half-track mounted battalion. Due to shortages of armored half-tracks, usually only a single Panzergrenadier battalion in each division was fully equipped with Sd.Kfz. 251 armored half-tracks **(1)**. So, at the beginning of July 1944, III./SS-Pz.Gren.Rgt. 4 had 98 armored half-tracks; the strength at the time of Operation *Lüttich* was much lower due to casualties suffered in the July fighting, especially the losses in the Roncey pocket during the Operation *Cobra* battles. The mounted Panzergrenadier attacks were frequently led by a Sd.Kfz. 251/9 Kanonenwagen, as seen here **(2)**. This was a fire support version of the half-track, fitted with a short-barreled 7.5cm gun.

Opposing SS-Pz.Gren.Rgt. 4 attack was Lt. Tom Springfield's 1st Platoon, Company A, 823rd Tank Destroyer Battalion, equipped with four 3in. M5 towed anti-tank guns **(3)**. This unit had arrived near Abbaye Blanche on the evening of August 6, and had enough time to survey the local terrain. Springfield positioned his four guns to cover the neighboring road intersections.

The SS-Pz.Gren.Rgt. 4 columns advanced in the morning fog with no real idea where the American defenses might be located. Springfield's guns began engaging the Das Reich columns as they became visible through the early morning fog around 0600hrs **(4)**. During the ensuing firefight, Springfield's unit claimed to have knocked out four half-tracks, three PzKpfw IV tanks, three cargo trucks, four armored cars, and 13 other vehicles. The Das Reich column dismounted some of its troops who attacked Springfield's positions on foot. They reached within a few dozen yards of the guns, so close that the gun crews used hand-grenades to repulse the attack. Neighboring US infantry engaged the German troops with .30-cal. machine guns and the initial attacks subsided.

staff managed to escape. They attempted to reach Hill 314, but were cut off by roving German infantry. They found refuge in another building where they remained hidden for the next two days until discovered on Wednesday August 9 when the battalion commander, Lt. Col. Hardaway and many of his staff were captured. I./SS-Pz.Gren.Rgt. 3 gained full control of the town of Mortain by 1000hrs.

Wisliceny's second column bypassed Mortain and headed further westward to the village of Romagny. Colonel Birks had sent the regimental I&R (Intelligence and Reconnaissance) Platoon to the town and they managed to hold off the first wave of Das Reich Panzergrendiers. They were forced to retreat when the remainder of the German column arrived before dawn.

The attack by Weidinger's SS-Pz.Gren.Rgt. 4. toward L'Abbaye Blanche had far less success than the southern group. Supported by one company of StuG III assault guns, the column was late in departing its staging area due to the traffic jam with 1. SS-Panzer-Division. As a result, Weidinger decided to try to seize its objectives using a half-track borne assault group formed from 9. Kompanie. In the early morning fog it encountered very few American troops. Weidinger's spearhead eventually ran into a roadblock established by Lt. Tom Springfield's 1st Platoon, Co. A, 823rd Tank Destroyer Battalion, reinforced by 57mm anti-tank guns of the Anti-tank Company, 120th Infantry embedded in an infantry platoon strongpoint led by Lt. Tom Andrew of Co. F, 120th Infantry. In total, the defensive positions contained about 70 men, but had been well surveyed by Lt. Springfield the day before to provide anti-tank gun coverage over the four roads in the immediate vicinity. Furthermore, the area had been prepared for defense by German troops who held the town earlier in the month, offering an existing network of trenches and strongpoints.

One of the most heavily contested sectors of the L'Abbaye Blanche road block was to the north around the Mortain–Le Neufbourg railway station where several roads converged. Lieutenant Tom Springfield's 1st Platoon, Co. A, 823rd Tank Destroyer Battalion was deployed in the woods to the northeast of the station with guns #3 and #4 to the west (1) and guns #1 and #2 on the east side of the woods (2). As can be seen, these four 3in. guns could cover much of the road network in the area. The station itself is identified here as (3). The knocked-out German column shown in several photos here along the tree-lined road is identified as (4).

This is a view of the aftermath of the fighting near the Mortain-Le Neufbourg railway station with a column of knocked-out vehicles from 2. SS-Panzer-Division including an Sd.Kfz. 251 Ausf. D armored half-track in the foreground and a Kettenkrad half-track motorcycle behind it. The train station can be seen in the background. The half-track was probably from 9. Kompanie, SS-Pz.Gren.Rgt.4.

This is a view of the same column but from further down the road from the Mortain-Le Neufbourg railway station. There is a destroyed German truck from the 2. Panzer-Division in the foreground, followed by a pile-up of wrecks including a Schwimmwagen on the left, and Kubelwagen in the center and a Jeep on the right, and finally the Sd.kfz. 251 half-track seen in the other photos of this scene.

As the German vehicles became visible through the fog, they were engaged by the anti-tank guns. By early morning, the road approaching L'Abbaye Blanche was littered with six burning German vehicles, largely stopping the attack for the moment. A portion of the 2nd Platoon, Co. F under Lt. Stewart joined the defenses later in the morning after their roadblock closer to Mortain had been compromised. They reinforced the southern approaches to the L'Abbaye Blanche roadblock from Wisliceny's SS-Pz.Gren.Rgt. 3 force.

Major-General Hobbs decided to commit Lt. Col. J.W. Lockett's 2nd Battalion, 117th Infantry, minus Co. G, to attempt to re-establish control of Mortain itself. They arrived on the northern side of the town around dawn, accompanied by eight M4 tanks of the 743rd Tank Battalion. The bulk of the battalion under Lt. Col. Lockett along with four tanks headed into town, but were unable to breach German defenses. These forces were used to secure the road network leading to the L'Abbaye Blanche roadblock. Company F, with four tanks, was sent down the road on the western side of town to reach Romagny and were unable to do so, but did manage to keep open the road near Neufbourg. Later in the day, Lockett deployed Co. E to reinforce the L'Abbaye Blanche roadblock.

At 1300hrs, due to Allied air attacks, Funck's 47. Panzer-Korps headquarters ordered Das Reich to hold the positions that had been gained and consolidate them. As a result, by the end of Monday, August 7, Das Reich had managed to secure the town of Mortain but had failed to gain control of Hill 314 or L'Abbaye Blanche. Hill 314 offered the 120th Infantry a vantage point over the surrounding terrain, and with two artillery forward observers in place on the heights, it would become the major hazard to Operation *Lüttich* since it could provide accurate and timely spotting for VII Corps' considerable artillery force. Das Reich penetrations beyond Mortain such as the advance by SS-Panzer-Regiment 2 down the southwest road to Hilaire-du-Harcouët came to a halt due to the stop order from 47. Panzer-Korps.

This is another view of the column destroyed near the Mortain-Le Neufbourg railway station taken from the direction of the station with the knocked-out Sd.Kfz. 251 in the right foreground.

LEIBSTANDARTE AT ST. BARTHÉLEMY, AUGUST 7

The 1. SS-Panzer-Division "LSSAH" was the last division to arrive for Operation *Lüttich* and only a small portion was ready to participate in the first day's attack. The main commitment by the Leibstandarte on Monday was SS-Pz.Gren.Rgt. 2 and parts of I./SS-Pz.Rgt. 1 that were sent to reinforce Kampfgruppe Brassert from the 2. Panzer-Division. Kampfgruppe Brassert, led by Oberst Karl Brassert, was based on Pz.Gren.Rgt. 2 supported by tanks from the 2. Panzer-Division. The main objective of this attack was the road junction at the village of St. Barthélemy. The battlegroup from the 2. Panzer-Division struck along the northern roads, while the Leibstandarte attacked from the east and south. While many accounts suggest that one of the Leibstandarte battlegroups was led by the famous Jochen Peiper, in

OPERATION *LÜTTICH* PANZER ATTACK, AUGUST 7, 1944 (PP. 42–43)

The spearheads in the attack of Operation *Lüttich* were the Panther tank battalions of four Panzer divisions taking part in the initial attack. Each Panzer regiment generally included two battalions, the I. Bataillon equipped with Panther tanks **(1)** and the II. Bataillon equipped with PzKpfw IV tanks. Of the approximately 250 tanks taking part at the start of Operation *Lüttich*, about 120 were Panthers. The Panthers were chosen to serve as the spearheads of the attack since they were better armored than the PzKpfw IV. Their frontal armor was essentially impervious to the most powerful US Army weapons of the time, the 3in. anti-tank guns and 76mm tank guns.

Although the Panther was largely invulnerable to American anti-tank guns from a purely frontal position, its side armor was far more modest and could be penetrated by any of the standard American anti-tank weapons, including the 57mm anti-tank gun and the 75mm tank gun. The heavy frontal armor of the Panther

was invaluable in mobile engagements when the crew could direct it like a shield against likely enemy positions. In *bocage* terrain conditions such as those found around Mortain, ambush from unexpected directions was more common.

Due to their use as the spearheads in the initial Operation *Lüttich* attack, the Panthers suffered a disproportionate share of the German tank casualties. Of the 50 tanks found after the battle, 34 were Panthers and only 16 were PzKpfw IV tanks. Of the Panther losses, 14 were knocked out by tank or anti-tank gun fire, five were knocked out by Typhoon **(2)** rockets, four were destroyed by their own crews, six were abandoned intact, and four were lost due to undetermined causes. The Typhoon rockets could not penetrate the thick frontal armor of the Panther, but rocket strikes tended to occur against the thinner top armor of the tank which could be collapsed by a combination of the rocket's impact speed and its high-explosive warhead.

fact he had suffered a breakdown from combat exhaustion a few days before and had been evacuated.

St. Barthélemy was held by Lt. Col. Robert Frankland's 1/117th Infantry. This unit had arrived in the village around noon on August 6, and had taken over positions previously held by the 26th Infantry, 1st Division. Frankland felt that the battalion's position was extremely exposed since the 3/117th Infantry was deployed behind his battalion to the northwest while the 2/117th had been detached in support of the 120th Infantry to the south in Mortain. The battalion was initially under the impression that they were going into an assembly area, and they were not informed that they were being sent to actually defend the village until shortly before their arrival. The 1/117th Infantry had Cos. A and C deployed in and around St. Barthélemy while Company B was in reserve to the northwest near the hamlet of Le Fantay.

Several of the Das Reich Panzergrenadier attacks were led by these Sd.Kfz. 251/9 Kanonenwagen. This was the standard medium armored half-track fitted with a short 7.5cm gun. The armor on these vehicles was adequate to stop small arms fire, but many were hit with anti-tank gun fire with catastrophic results as seen here.

The Leibstandarte attack began unevenly in the early morning hours of August 7 due to the late arrival of its units. A scouting party approached St. Barthélemy around midnight, followed shortly after by a small group of tanks. The tanks engaged the forward roadblock, consisting of a couple of infantry squads and a 57mm anti-tank gun. The anti-tank gun was knocked out, and the infantry withdrew a few hundred yards to the south of the road. Divisional artillery engaged the German tanks, halting the attack for the time being.

The main attack took place at 0600hrs with columns advancing down all three roads leading into St. Barthélemy. Due to the fog, the tanks were able to approach the American defenses to nearly point-blank ranges before they were seen. The Co. A roadblock toward La Sablonnière was quickly overrun as was the Co. C outpost further west. Frankland was in radio contact with

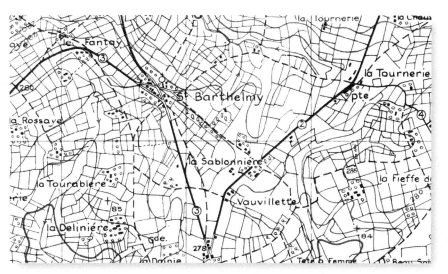

Vehicle movement in the Mortain area was constricted by the extensive *bocage* terrain, seen here on this contemporary US Army 1:25,000 scale map. The grid squares here are 1,000m across. This is the St. Barthélemy area, and road junction RJ278 can be seen at the bottom center of this map segment.

A cluster of knocked-out vehicles between Chérencé-le-Roussel and St. Barthélemy. In the foreground is a Panther Ausf. A of 3./SS-Pz.Rgt. 1 and behind it is a knocked-out M10 3in. GMC tank destroyer.

Another view of this same scene shows a pair of knocked out Panthers of 3./SS-Pz.Rgt. 1 with an Sd.Kfz. 251 Ausf. D. armored half-track in the foreground. The Operational Research team that investigated this site concluded that one of the Panthers was knocked out by gunfire, and the other by an aircraft rocket hit against its drive sprocket which led to crew abandonment of the tank.

both companies and told them to allow the German tanks to pass through and then deal with the accompanying infantry. Frankland later admitted that if he had appreciated the scale of the attack, he would have withdrawn his unit back to a more defensible position.

Besides having to deal with the Leibstandarte attacks, the town was suddenly hit by an influx of tanks and vehicles from Kampfgruppe Brassert from the northern road. Within moments, the German tanks had surrounded Frankland's command post in a house in St. Barthelemy. The senior officers went toward the back of the house to see what was happening, only to see two of the command post radiomen being led away by German troops. Frankland and a few of the other officers pushed through the back door and Frankland shot with his pistol two Germans who were confronting him. Frankland and the command staff then tried to arrange a defense by a platoon in the area, but seeing the number of tanks in town they realized this was futile. Instead, they raced back to the Co. B positions outside town to try to re-establish radio contact with the two forward companies.

These two forward companies withdrew in a haphazard fashion over the next few hours after having suffered severe casualties. By afternoon, about 25 men of Co. A and about 55 men from Co. C had reached the new defense line; both companies had a nominal strength of about 180 men each. These squads had managed to extricate themselves after Allied fighter-bombers started appearing over the town around noon, largely paralyzing the German attack.

A view of this field from yet another angle shows the destroyed Panther in the center, the Sd.Kfz. 251 to the right and the M10 3in. GMC to the left. The Operational Research investigation of these wrecks concluded that the half-track had been destroyed by a high-explosive projectile hit in the center, but it was not clear whether this was an aircraft rocket or field artillery.

The arrival of Allied aircraft completely altered the tempo of the battle. A Panzergrenadier from SS-Pz.Gren.Rgt. 2 recalled the arrival of the Allied fighter-bombers:

> Our Panzers halted on an asphalt road. We weren't moving forward. We riflemen sat on the Panzers. Luckily, there was thick fog. They must think that we're still in Russia where you can get away with big groups of Panzers like this. But today, German fighters were supposed to keep the air space above the attack free of enemy planes. We got off the Panzers as they moved off the road into the fields and tried to camouflage themselves. The fog broke. There weren't any German aircraft; there were only Allied planes. We cursed Hermann's Luftwaffe. If he wasn't going to fly today, when would he fly?
>
> The Jabos [Allied fighter-bombers] circled our tanks several times. Then one broke out of the circle, found its target and fired. As the first returned to

This Panther Ausf. A of SS-Pz. Rgt. 1 ran off the road, knocking over a telephone pole.

ABOVE LEFT
A burned-out Panther Ausf. A of SS-Pz.Rgt. 1 in the St. Barthélemy area after the fighting. About 15 Panthers of this unit were discovered in this area after the fighting along with two PzKpfw IVs.

ABOVE RIGHT
These Leibstandarte vehicles were apparently knocked out on the road between Juvigny-le-Tertre and St. Barthélemy. To the left is an Sd.Kfz. 251 Ausf. D armored half-track and to the right is a Volkswagen Schwimmwagen.

the circle of about 20 planes, a second pulled out of formation and fired. And so it continued until they all had fired. They left a terrible scene behind. A second swarm of Jabos appeared and fired all their rockets. They had it well organized!

Black clouds of smoke from burning fuel curled into the sky wherever we looked. It was the sign of a dead Panzer. There were dozens of smoke columns from our area alone. Finally, the Typhoons couldn't find any more tanks, so they swooped down on us and chased us mercilessly.

In the face of the Typhoon attacks, the attack ground to a halt by the early afternoon. Reinforcement for the St. Barthélemy assault was prevented by continued Allied air attacks. A large column of tanks and other vehicles from 2. Panzer-Division and the Leibstandarte were hit on the roads from St. Clement to St. Barthélemy in the afternoon of August 7. Aside from the equipment losses, these attacks also killed the commander of Pz.Rgt. 3, 2. Panzer-Division, Major Ferdinand Schneider-Kostalski.

KAMPFGRUPPE SCHAKE AT LE MESNIL-ADELÉE

The second main concentration of the 2. Panzer-Division was Kampfgruppe Schake. This was a mixed formation containing elements of the 2. Panzer-Division, 116. Panzer-Division and the Leibstandarte. This battlegroup was led by Oberst Hans Schacke, commander of Pz.Gren.Rgt. 304. The battlegroup consisted of four companies from his regiment supported by 18 Panther tanks of I./Pz.Rgt. 24 of 116. Panzer-Division, two companies of tank destroyers from Pz.Jg.Abt. 38, and three companies of SS-Panzeraufklarungs. Abt. 1 (SS-AA. 1). The objective of this formation was the small village of Le Mesnil-Adelée. This battlegroup made the deepest penetration of all the *Lüttich* formations, largely because they struck in an area where there was a wide gap in the American defenses.

The Leibstandarte reconnaissance battalion, SS-AA. 1, reached the small hamlet of Le Mesnil-Tôve in the dark around 0400hrs. There was at least one 57mm anti-tank gun as well as about a dozen trucks from the 12th Infantry, 4th Division in the town. The German troops dismounted, and infiltrated into town, quickly capturing it. At this point, Rittmeister Weidemann's Panther company, 4./Pz.Rgt. 24, as well as some of the tank destroyers of

Pz.Jg.Abt. 38 broke off from this formation and headed up the road toward Chérencé-le-Roussel to support the attack on that town by other elements of the 116. Panzer-Division.

The main column proceeded through town to the main objective at Le Mesnil-Adelée. This town was along the boundary between the 9th Infantry Division to the north and the 30th Division to the south and was not defended by American troops. Kampfgruppe Schake encircled the village and occupied it before dawn.

The 119th Infantry, in 30th Division reserve, dispatched Co. B to Le Mesnil-Adelée around dawn. It set up a roadblock with a pair of 57mm anti-tank guns to the southwest of the village after dawn. In the meantime, Lt. Col. Brown's 3rd Battalion, 119th Infantry was sent from its bivouac area eastward with an aim to retaking Le Mesnil-Tôve from the south. It passed through Juvigny-le-Tertre around 1100hrs with Co. I detaching from the battalion and heading off separately to the southeastern side of Le Mesnil-Adelée. The first attempt to take Le Mesnil-Tôve by Cos. K and L was repulsed and one of the accompanying tanks from a platoon of C/743rd Tank Battalion was knocked out. In the meantime, Co. I reached Le Mesnil-Adelée and set up a defensive perimeter on the south side of the village.

The first major intervention by American tanks in this sector was unplanned. The 67th Armored Regiment, 2nd Armored Division was also in the area for rehabilitation after Operation *Cobra*. On the morning of August 7, it was conducting a 55-mile administrative road march from Pont Brocard to Domfront via Chérencé-le-Roussel and Mortain. While moving south near Le Mesnil-Gilbert, the advance party under Lt. Finley of Co. G, 67th Armored, spotted enemy activity to its front which was Kampfgruppe Schake in Le Mesnil-Adelée. Finley's tank company, supported by the M7 105mm HMC self-propelled howitzers of the 78th Armored Field Artillery Battalion (AFAB) was sent to attack the German force, followed later by Co. C and a platoon from the 702nd Tank Destroyer Battalion. In the fog, the two groups exchanged long-range fire, with the 67th Armored claiming four

On the morning of August 7, CCB, 3rd Armored Division dispatched Task Force King from their refitting area near Reffuveille to attack Kampfgruppe Schake at Le Mesnil-Adelée. The medium tanks here are from Cos. F to the left and Co. I to the right, with the M3 half-tracks of Co. I, 36th Armored Infantry evident along the tree line.

US UNITS

2nd Armored Division
A. 67th Armored Regiment
3rd Armored Division
B. Task Force King
4th Infantry Division
C. 3/8th Infantry
D. 1/39th Infantry
30th Infantry Division
E. Co. B, 1st Battalion, 119th Infantry
F. Cos. K and L, 3rd Battalion, 119th Infantry
G. Co. I, 3rd Battalion, 119th Infantry

2 BROOKS

3 WATSON

30 HOBBS

LE MESNIL-GILBER

LE MESNIL-ADELÉE

EVENTS

1. Kampfgruppe Schake includes four Panzergrenadier companies from Oberst Hans Schake's Pz.Gren.Rgt. 304 supported by 18 Panther tanks of I./Pz.Rgt. 24 of 116. Panzer-Division, two companies of tank destroyers of Pz.Jg.Abt. 38, and three companies of SS-Panzeraufklarungs.Abt. 1. The objective of this formation is the small village of Le Mesnil-Adelée.

2. The Leibstandarte reconnaissance battalion, SS-Panzeraufklarungs.Abt. 1, reaches the small hamlet of Le Mesnil-Tôve in the dark around 0400hrs capturing about a dozen trucks from the 12th Infantry, 4th Division. The German troops dismount and infiltrate into town, quickly capturing it.

3. Rittmeister Weidemann's Panther company, 4./Pz.Rgt. 24, as well as some of the tank destroyers of Pz.Jg.Abt. 38 break off from the main formation and head up the road toward Chérencé-le-Roussel to support the attack on that town by other elements of the 116. Panzer-Division.

4. The 119th Infantry dispatch Co. B to Le Mesnil-Adelée around dawn to set up a roadblock with a pair of 57mm anti-tank guns to the southwest of the village.

5. Lieutenant-Colonel Brown's 3rd Battalion, 119th Infantry is sent from its bivouac area eastward with an aim to retaking Le Mesnil-Tôve from the south. It passes through Juvigny-le-Tertre around 1100hrs. The first attempt to take Le Mesnil-Tôve by Cos. K and L, 3/119th Infantry is repulsed and one of the accompanying tanks from a platoon of C/743rd Tank Battalion knocked out.

6. In the meantime, Co. I has detached from the rest of 3/119th Infantry, headed toward Le Mesnil-Adelée and set up a defensive perimeter on the southeast edge of the village.

7. The 67th Armored Regiment, 2nd Armored Division begins a 55-mile (90km) road march to Domfront via Chérencé-le-Roussel and Mortain. After spotting enemy activity in Le Mesnil-Adelée it exchanges long-range fire with Kampfgruppe Schake, killing the German battlegroup commander, Oberst Schake.

8. In the later part of the morning, the 3/8th Infantry, 4th Division moves into Le Mesnil-Adelée. As a result, the 3/67th Armored breaks off the engagement with Kampfgruppe Schake. In view of the enemy activity on its intended route, the 67th Armored Regiment reverses course and heads to Domfront along roads further west.

9. In the late morning, a dozen P-47D Thunderbolts of the 50th Fighter Group attack Kampfgruppe Schake, claiming to have knocked out six tanks but actually only damaging a few of them.

10. As the fog departs around noon, Kampfgruppe Schanke gets a better view of the American defenses and stages a counter-attack against the Co. I positions.

11. Combat Command B, 3rd Armored Division is assigned to support the 30th Division to repulse the German offensive. This mission of retaking Le Mesnil-Adelée is assigned to Col. Dorrance Roysdon's 33rd Armored Regiment. Roysdon puts together a task force under Col. King including three tank companies from 33rd Armored.

12. Company F, 33rd Armored is assigned to conduct the attack into Le Mesnil-Adelée. A two-pronged attack collapses the German defenses, and the acting *Kampfgruppe* commander, Major Kuno von Meyer orders Kampfgruppe Schake to retreat back to Le Mesnil-Tôve around 1700hrs.

13. The American tanks do not pursue but clear out the village with the help of the armored infantry company.

14. As Kampfgruppe Schake heads eastward, the column is spotted by an artillery observation plane of the 4th Infantry Division, which directs fire from the 155mm howitzers of the 20th Field Artillery Battalion against it, destroying many trucks and support vehicles.

KAMPFGRUPPE SCHAKE AT LE MESNIL-ADELÉE, AUGUST 7

GERMAN UNITS
1. Kampfgruppe Schake
2. SS-Panzeraufklarungs.Abt. 1
3. Kampfgruppe Zander

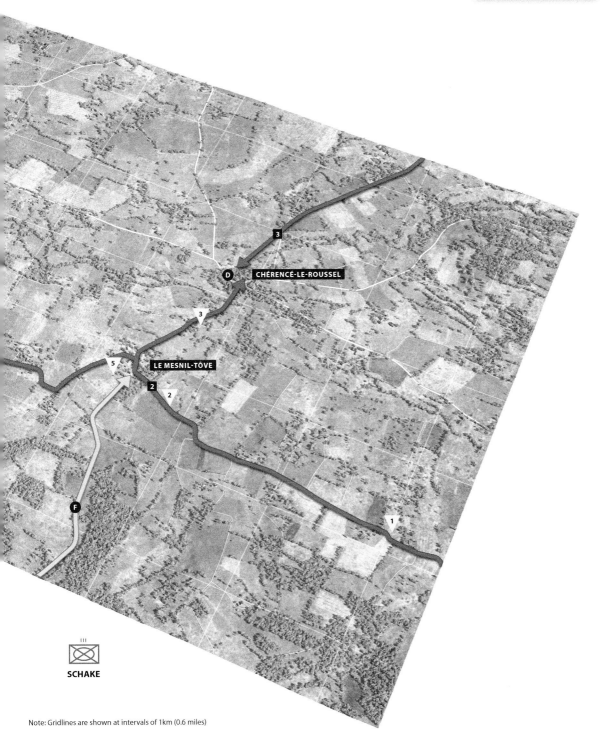

SCHAKE

Note: Gridlines are shown at intervals of 1km (0.6 miles)

This is an M4 medium tank of the HQ Platoon, of Lt. Carter's Co. I, 33rd Armored Regiment, CCB, 3rd Armored Division on August 7, 1944 during the attack toward Le Mesnil-Adelée. It is carrying "armored doughs" of Co. I, 36th Armored Infantry Regiment. This tank was knocked out two days later on August 9, 1944 when hit by German gunfire, starting an ammunition fire.

German tanks. During the engagement, howitzer fire from the 78th AFAB killed the German battlegroup commander, Oberst Schake, and command was taken over by Major Kuno von Meyer. In the later part of the morning, the 3/8th Infantry, 4th Division moved into Le Mesnil-Gilbert. As a result, the 3/67th Armored broke off the engagement and continued on its road march to Domfront, skirting around Le Mesnil-Adelée far to the west.

The first Allied fighter-bombers reached this area in the late morning. A dozen P-47D Thunderbolts of the 50th Fighter Group attacked Kampfgruppe Schake, claiming to have knocked out six tanks, but actually only damaged a few tanks. Regardless of the actual damage, the air attacks, as well as the increasing appearance of US troops, discouraged any further advance. The situation in the area was so confused that the P-47s strafed the I/119th Infantry positions south of the village, and some of the 67th Armored tanks were damaged by rocket-firing Typhoons.

As the fog departed, Kampfgruppe Schanke got a better view of the American defenses. Three Panther tanks with accompanying infantry disrupted the Co. I, 119th Infantry positions southeast of the village, but the stalemate continued.

Due to the Ultra decrypts late on the night of August 6–7, VII Corps was alerted to the German offensive and began mobilizing forces for a possible counter-attack. The 3rd Armored Division was in the area, conducting maintenance and repair. In the early morning hours, the division was alerted for probable commitment. Combat Command A (CCA) under Brig. Gen. Doyle Hickey had already been ordered to deploy toward Mayenne, so around 0700hrs, Col. Truman Boudinot's CCB was assigned to support the 30th Division. The major German attacks had halted by mid-morning, except for the penetration at Le Mesnil-Adelée. As a result, Hobbs instructed Boudinot to send a force to block any further penetration in that area. This

mission was assigned to Col. Dorrance Roysdon's 33rd Armored Regiment. Roysdon put together a task force under Col. King. The tank element included three companies from 33rd Armored, including Capt. McGeorge's Co. A of M5A1 light tanks and two medium tank companies, each with 17 M4 tanks, Capt. McMann's Co. F and Lt. Carter's Company I of the 33rd Armored, a company of the 36th Armored Infantry Regiment, and smaller detachments of tank destroyers, reconnaissance and engineers.

Company F, 33rd Armored was assigned to conduct the attack into Le Mesnil-Adelée. Supporting field artillery first began to hit the village with high-explosive, switching to smoke immediately before the attack to conceal the approaching American tanks. Two tank platoons conducted an attack directly into the village from the south while the third platoon attacked from the north. The attack from the south attracted the most attention and took the heaviest casualties, losing four tanks. The arrival of the 3rd Platoon from the north was a complete surprise to the German defenders and several Panthers were knocked out or damaged in the initial exchange. With the American tanks about to overwhelm his defenses, Major Kuno von Meyer ordered Kampfgruppe Schake to retreat back to Le Mesnil-Tôve around 1700hrs. Meyer and his adjutant were seriously wounded by artillery; Meyer was later awarded the Knight's Cross for his leadership that day. German casualties in the fighting are unclear. One 116. Panzer-Division history puts the losses as four Panthers; various American after-action reports claimed six to 15 Panthers.

The American tanks did not pursue but cleared out the village with the help of the armored infantry company. As Kampfgruppe Schake headed eastward, the column was spotted by an artillery observation plane of the 4th Infantry Division which directed fire from the 155mm howitzers of the 20th Field Artillery Battalion against it. This led to more casualties, mostly the unarmored trucks and support vehicles, but at least two Sd.Kfz. 251 armored half-tracks were also destroyed.

This is a sunken road near Chérencé-le-Roussel with the wreckage of several Sd.Kfz. 251 armored half-tracks and other vehicles of the 116. Panzer-Division knocked out in the fighting.

116. PANZER-DIVISION: CHÉRENCÉ-LE-ROUSSEL

The northernmost element of the *Lüttich* attack was conducted by a battlegroup of the 116. Panzer-Division. The scale of this attack was limited by confusion over the division's mission. The 116. Panzer-Division was supposed to be relieved by the newly arriving 84. Infanterie-Division. However, the new division was inexperienced and under heavy pressure from attacking US forces pushing toward Sourdeval. A US Army advance toward Gathemo forced 116. Panzer-Division to commit one of its two Panzergrenadier regiments to the fight, and it also had its divisional artillery and tank destroyer battalion supporting the 84. Infanterie-Division at the outset of Operation *Lüttich*. Its Panzer element had already been taken away to support the 2. Panzer-Division south of the Sée River. As a result, its attack force was limited to Kampgruppe Zander, led by Oberstleutnant Helmut Zander, commander of Pz.Gren.Rgt. 60. The force included his regiment reinforced by one battalion from Pz.Gren.Rgt. 156. It was assigned to capture the small village of Chérencé-le-Roussel.

A camouflaged 57mm anti-tank position of the 1/39th Infantry, 9th Division in position along a road in Chérencé-le-Roussel on August 9.

The village was held by the 1st Battalion, 39th Infantry, 9th Infantry Division with a platoon of tanks from the 746th Tank Battalion. This battalion had been in the area for three days and had been attempting to capture the hills to the immediate east of the village.

A pair of German motorcycles on a scouting mission stumbled into American outposts at 2230hrs on Sunday night, August 6, but were knocked out. The American defenses had been alerted to the German attack by all of the noise from Kampfgruppe Schake that was passing to the immediate south near Le Mesnil-Tôve. The attack by Kampfgruppe Zander began around 0200hrs from the direction of Mont Turgon,

A 60mm mortar crew of the 39th Infantry, 9th Division in mid-August 1944. Each infantry company had a heavy weapons platoon with three of these mortars. As seen on the troops here, the 39th Infantry in Normandy painted their helmets with the A-A-A-O "Triple-A Bar Nothing" marking.

immediately east of the village. The dismounted infantry attack pushed back the American defenses but failed to secure the village. As a result, Kampfgruppe Zander requested tank support and Rittmeister Weidemann's Panther company, 4./Pz.Rgt. 24, as well as some of the tank destroyers of Pz.Jg.Abt. 38, broke off from Kampfgruppe Schake to the south and headed up the road toward Chérencé-le-Roussel. A counter-attack at 0445hrs by Co. C, 39th Infantry regained much of the ground it had lost previously, and the German tanks were not able to decisively influence the fighting due to the lack of decent roads and constricted *bocage* terrain. After daybreak, other elements of the 39th Infantry were sent into the area as reinforcement along with Co. B, 8th Infantry, 4th Division.

The commander of the 39th Infantry since the Sicily campaign in 1943 was the legendary Col. Harry "Paddy" Flint. He had originated the "Triple-A Bar Nothing" marking as a morale booster for his unit based on his slogan for the regiment "Anything, Anytime, Anywhere, bar none!". Flint was killed in combat during the hedgerow fighting on July 24 and command was taken over by his executive officer, Lt. Col. Van H. Bond, seen here on the left.

The failure of Kampfgruppe Zander to capture Chérencé-le-Roussel led to another angry telephone exchange between corps commander Baron Funck and the commander of the 116. Panzer-Division, Graf von Schwerin. Funck accused the division of cowardice and Schwerin angrily responded that "I will not allow myself or my division to be insulted." Instead of contacting Hausser, who had refused to relieve Schwerin the evening before, Funck contacted Kluge and insisted on his relief. This was put in motion and Oberst Walter Reinhardt, the chief of staff of the 47. Panzer-Korps, was put in temporary command on the morning of August 8.

MONDAY AUGUST 7: THE DAY OF THE TYPHOON

Early morning fog kept Allied airpower from intervening in the Mortain area until noon. The RAF's 2nd Tactical Air Force sent a patrol of two Typhoons from 121 Wing to Mortain in late morning, finding the area shrouded in low fog and clouds. After finding a gap in the cover, the Typhoons discovered a column nearly five miles (8km) long heading westward and radioed for more aircraft to follow. The first Typhoon squadrons departed their bases shortly after noon and began conducting rocket attacks in the St. Barthelémy and Cheréncé area. The strikes by 121 and 124 Wings hit mainly in the northern portions of the German attack. 84 Group attempted to make strikes against Das Reich in the Mortain area, but low cloud cover and fog limited these attacks for most of Monday. In total, 2 TAF conducted 305 Typhoon sorties on August 7, claiming 90 tanks destroyed and 59 damaged along with 51 vehicles. Monday was later dubbed "The Day of the Typhoon."

The USAAF XIX Tactical Air Command conducted 601 sorties on August 7, of which about 400 were in the Mortain battle area. Total claims for the day included 12–13 tanks, 98 trucks and 90 horse-drawn vehicles. The tank kills all came from seven rocket-armed P-47s of 406th Group that also claimed four half-tracks, five staff cars, and four light Flak positions, firing about 600 rockets.

As promised, the Luftwaffe's Jagdkorps 2 made an attempt to provide air support for the *Lüttich* attack. The mission plan consisted both of ground-attack sorties as well as fighter sweeps intended to keep Allied fighters at bay. Due to the ground fog, the attacks were postponed until 1400hrs with a wave of attacks by six *Gruppen*. A mission by six rocket-armed Fw 190A-8s escorted by 18 Bf 109G-6s of Jagdgeschwader 26 was spotted by P-47s which claimed 12 victories in the ensuing dogfights. Jagdgeschwader 26 losses were actually five aircraft, but other German formations may have been involved. A string of dogfights erupted around the German airbases near Chartres, which seriously limited the number of Luftwaffe aircraft reaching the Avranches/Mortain area. P-51s of the 354th Group strafed one field east of Chartres, claiming 12 Bf 109s and one Ju 88 bomber on the ground, but losing three fighters to Flak. An attack by P-47s of 36th Group against another Chartres airfield claimed six more Luftwaffe aircraft. By the end of the day, XIX TAC claimed 14 German aircraft in the air and 19 on the ground for a loss of ten US fighters, mainly to Flak.

Hill 314 dominated the countryside around Mortain with vistas as far away as the Atlantic coast. This is a view of the hill from the southwest.

The Luftwaffe missions continued into the early evening. The 120th Infantry in the Mortain area reported at least ten sorties against their positions, mainly by rocket-firing Fw 190A-8 fighters. In total, Jagdkorps 2 conducted 128 sorties that day, well short of the 300 promised, or the 1,000 sorties demanded by Berlin.

Although Allied air power clearly had a major impact on the Mortain fighting, there has been some controversy regarding how large a role it played in the initial German setbacks. The kill claims by 2 TAF and IX TAC were high enough that the Operational Research Sections (ORS) from both the 21st Army Group and 2 TAF decided to conduct a survey of the battlefield on August 12–20, 1944 to quantify the extent of damage. The results are summarized in the accompanying chart. As can be seen, the number of tanks and armored vehicles actually knocked out by air attack was substantially less than claimed. Of the 21 AFVs that ORS attributed to aircraft, 15 were due to rockets, four to cannon or machine-gun fire and two to bombs. According to the ORS survey, about a quarter of the AFV kills could be attributed to aircraft attack. The largest number of AFVs were attributed to anti-tank guns or tank gun fire. There were a large number of vehicles so badly damaged that the cause was unclear, especially trucks and other soft-skin vehicles and many of these were probably due to air attack.

Target	Air attack	Abandoned	US Army	Unknown	Total
Panther	6	10	14	3	33
PzKpfw IV	3	1	5	1	10
SP gun	0	0	1	2	3
APC	11	1	3	8	23
Armored car	1	1	5	1	8
Vehicles	12	5	7	26	50
Total	33	18	35	41	127

Regardless of the actual number of vehicles lost to air attack, the battlefield impact of the air attacks was substantial. Numerous German accounts attribute the air attacks to the halt in Operation *Lüttich* around 1300hrs

DAY OF THE TYPHOON, AUGUST 7, 1944 (PP. 58–59)

August 7, 1944 became known as "The Day of the Typhoon" due to the dramatic impact of the Typhoon **(1)** attacks against the German tank columns around Mortain. The principal anti-tank weapon used by the Typhoons was the RP-3, an abbreviation for Rocket Projectile 3 Inch **(2)**. The 3in. referred to the diameter of the rocket motor. The RP-3 was first used for tank-busting in the Desert Campaign in early 1943. The 25-pound armor-piercing warheads were found to be ineffective against the Tiger tanks encountered in Tunisia in early 1943. As a result, a new 60-pound semi-armor-piercing (SAP) warhead was introduced which contained 12 pounds of high explosive. The rockets weighed 82 pounds (37kg) and were 55in. long. They had a maximum speed of 1,600 feet per second (480m/s) and an effective range of 1,700 yards (1,600m). The Typhoon carried four rocket rail launchers under each wing for a total of eight rockets. Using a selector switch, the pilot could fire the rockets singly, in pairs, or in a full salvo.

As mentioned in the text, pilot claims for knocked-out tanks proved to be significantly exaggerated when Operational Research Sections visited the battlefields. In reality, the rockets were not especially accurate. In addition, the Typhoon pilot typically pulled up the aircraft after rocket launch, and so never saw the actual rocket impact. Regardless of the precise number of tanks knocked out by rocket impacts, the Typhoon attacks had a devastating impact on German morale. Later interrogations of captured German tank crews revealed that "the German tank crews are extremely frightened of attacks by RP [rocket projectiles]… Crews are very aware that if an RP does hit a tank, their chance of survival is small. It is admitted that the chances of a direct hit are slight; nevertheless, this would hardly be appreciated by a crew whose first thought would be of the disastrous results if a hit was obtained." The demoralizing effects of air attack frequently prompted Panzer units to halt their operations and drive their vehicles to the shelter of hedgerows to escape attack. Some tank crews in more exposed locations appear to have abandoned their vehicles. The attacks were decisive due to their demoralizing and disruptive effects.

on August 7, 1944. For example, Hans Speidel, chief of staff of Heeresgruppe B, later remarked that "it was possible for the Allied air forces alone to wreck this Panzer operation with the help of a well-coordinated ground-to-air communications system." General der Panzertruppen Heinrich Freiherr von Lüttwitz, commander of 2. Panzer-Division during the battle, later wrote that "They came in hundreds, firing their rockets at the concentrated tanks and vehicles. We could do nothing against them and we could make no further progress." From a tactical standpoint, this disruption in the Panzer operations was a vital consequence of the air attack, paralyzing the Panzer operations on the early afternoon of August 7 when a breakthrough of the US infantry defenses remained a possibility. Once the momentum of the attack was broken that day, the chances for the success of Operation *Lüttich* declined precipitously since the US Army could push far greater forces into the battlezone than could the Wehrmacht.

This overhead view shows the northern section of Hill 314. The town of Mortain was to the left of this photo. As can be seen, the hill was not easily accessible from the western side due to the cliffs. The most frequent avenue for attack by the Germans was the small road evident in the lower right, which provided some possibilities for armored vehicle support.

HILL 314

Funck authorized a renewal of the offensive after nightfall on August 7 on the presumption that Allied air attacks would cease. Some sporadic fighting occurred, including artillery shelling by both sides. Large-scale fighting did not resume until Tuesday, August 8.

The 30th Division was in a precarious position since its forces were scattered across a wide and disconnected front. The most dangerous situation was the "Lost Battalion," the 2/120th Infantry, trapped on top of Hill 314 on the eastern side of Mortain. Since Das Reich was in control of the town of Mortain, the loss of Hill 314 would collapse the southern flank of the 30th Division and create a gap between the 30th Division and other VII Corps units to the south around Barenton. The situation on Hill 314 was jeopardized by the dispersal of the individual companies due to infiltration by Kampfgruppe 17 the day before. The defenses on Hill 314 were based on three companies and were triangular in layout. Company K held the northern portion of the hill while the southern base of the triangle consisted of Co. E to the east and Co. G to the west. Besides the three companies, there were small elements from Cos. C, H, and I on the hill. Overall command of the forces on the hilltop was under Capt. Reynold C. Erichson of Co. F.

There is some confusion regarding the name for this hill. Various US Army accounts refer to it as either Hill 314 or Hill 317. The source of the confusion was the different maps in use at the time. The widely used 1:25,000 US Army map identified it as Hill 314. However, the 1:50,000 US Army map correctly shows two high points. The southern peak, where Le Petit Chapelle is located, was identified as Hill 314; the second peak further to the northeast was identified as Hill 317. In this book, the Hill 314 identification is used; the hill is known as Montjoie by local French inhabitants.

Most of the initial German attacks were directed against the eastern side of the hill. Even after the capture of the town of Mortain on August 7, there were few attacks from the western side because of the presence of a broad stone cliff in that direction. There was a single east–west road toward the southern side of the hill which was a frequent avenue of German attacks since it permitted the use of armored vehicle support. The defensive positions on Hill 314 enjoyed natural advantages. The hilltop was punctuated by numerous large boulders and rock outcroppings that offered some natural defensive positions and shelter from German artillery fire. Most importantly, the hill offered a superb vista over the entire surrounding area. There were two radio-equipped, forward observer teams from the 230th Field Artillery Battalion as well as an observer team from the regimental 120th Cannon Company. Due to the importance of retaining Hill 314, the forward observers were given special priority by VII Corps artillery for fire missions.

Kampfgruppe Fick made three attempts to overrun Hill 314 in the pre-dawn hours of August 8, presuming that the artillery would be less accurate in the dark. However, the forward observers had already pre-registered several obvious avenues of approach, and the attacks were crushed.

The 2/120th Infantry was seriously short of ammunition, especially for crew-served weapons such as machine guns and mortars. A request was radioed to division headquarters for an air-drop, but confusion between division and corps led to a long delay in preparing an airdrop. In the meantime, 30th Division artillery attempted to assist the 2/120th by dropping supplies from their light spotter aircraft. Two aircraft made low altitude passes over the hill in the morning but suffered serious damage from German small arms fire and 2cm Flak automatic cannon. This put an end to this method of re-supply.

A new problem arose during the day when one of the two forward observer teams lost their radio connection after their available supply of dry-cell batteries became exhausted. This left only a single channel of communication between the "Lost Battalion" and the 30th Division, via Lt. Robert Weiss' team.

The Operation *Lüttich* attack had placed very little emphasis on artillery support, and this shortcoming became very evident on August 8 when Kampfgruppe 17 tried to capture Hill 31. The 17. Panzergrenadier-Division had very little surviving artillery of its own, and indeed many of the gunners had been converted to improvised infantry serving with Kampfgruppe 17. The remainder of its artillery strength, ten 10.5cm lFH 18/40s and nine 15cm sFH 18s, were consolidated under Artillerie-Gruppe Ernst in an effort to smother the American resistance on Hill 314. This effort got off to a bad start when the German forward observer team in a pair of Kubelwagens stumbled into an American ambush at the foot of Hill 314 with the observer being captured. He revealed that Artillerie-Gruppe Ernst was deployed near Ger, so Lt. Weiss was able to get corps artillery to conduct a counter-battery strike against the German artillery. Later in the day, Das Reich shifted a small number of self-propelled guns to support Kampfgruppe 17, but these were spotted by Weiss's team and forced to disperse when struck by counter-battery fire. After the early morning attacks, German infantry assaults on Hill 314 diminished due to the heavy casualties and exhaustion of the troops of Kampfgruppe Fick.

While Kampfgruppe Fick attempted to overrun Hill 314, the other Kampfgruppe 17 group, Kampfgruppe Ullrich, attempted to clear the American defenders behind Mortain on Hill 285. In the early morning hours of August 7–8, a German assault team including Pionier flamethrowers, attempted to rout the anti-tank guns and Co. B defenses by infiltrating into the positions under the cover of darkness. This group was discovered before they could reach the main defenses, and the attack was broken up. A second attack, spearheaded by Das Reich PzKpfw IV tanks, made another try around 0600hrs. The German infantry failed to accompany the tanks. One of the PzKpfw IV tanks ran over a mine and two others were knocked out by a concealed 3in. anti-tank gun about 50 yards from the main defense line; the remainder retreated. During a subsequent early morning attack, US artillery support fell short and landed within the American defenses, forcing the anti-tank gun teams to find shelter. Kampfgruppe Ulrich exploited this situation and managed to penetrate the Co. B defenses using a captured US Sherman tank. Nevertheless, the American artillery fire stripped away many of the accompanying German infantry, and the attack faltered. This sector remained quiet for the rest of August 8, but Kampfgruppe Ullrich launched another attack after dark around 2300hrs, which failed to make any inroads. By this stage, Kampfgruppe 17 was short of armored support and so was reinforced by a platoon of Panther tanks from I./SS-Pz.Rgt. 2 for another attack around midnight on August 8–9.

Weidinger's SS-Pz.Gren.Rgt. 4 made another attempt at overcoming the L'Abbaye Blanche roadblock on the morning of August 8, spearheading the attack with a pair of Kanonenwagen, Sd.Kfz. 251/9 half-tracks armed with a 7.5cm gun. These approached the cross-roads in the early morning fog but were spotted by the 3in. anti-tank guns and knocked out. Subsequent infantry attacks, including the use of flamethrowers, were beaten back. The attacks subsided for a time when the morning fog lifted and the Typhoons returned. SS-Panzergrenadier-Regiment 4 made another attempt near the south end of the roadblock in mid-afternoon without success.

The countryside around Mortain was dominated by *bocage*, fields edged with high hedgerows. This shows two riflemen of Co. A, 1/119th Infantry in action along the base of a hedgerow during the fighting around Romagny with the Das Reich division on August 9.

SOUTH OF MORTAIN

The bulk of the Das Reich, including Wisliceny's SS-Pz.Gren.Rgt. 3 as well as the division's Panzer regiment and reconnaissance battalion were deployed to the southwest of Mortain in an arc facing toward St. Hilaire-du-Harcouët, the division's intermediate objective. Hausser, the 7. Armee commander, visited the Das Reich command post at 1000hrs on August 8 to discuss plans with Otto Baum, the Das Reich commander. Hausser informed him that additional forces were on their way, and in the meantime, the division took up a largely defensive orientation during the daylight hours, confining attacks to dawn and dusk when air attack was less likely.

The 2/117th Infantry continued in its attempts to reach and secure Romagny from the northeast. This was a hopeless task in view of the enormous disparity in forces. This sector remained a stalemate for nearly four days due to the Das Reich's defenses in the area between Mortain and Romagny. Likewise, the 1/119th Infantry attempted to push out of Romagny to the northeast to relieve the 2/120th Infantry trapped on Hill 314. The battalion was supported by D Co. from the 743rd Tank Battalion, equipped with M5A1 light tanks, with two attached M4 medium tanks and a M4 dozer tank. The battalion attempted to move out toward Mortain on the mid-afternoon of August 8, but immediately was stopped by tank gun fire from the Das Reich perimeter located southwest of Mortain. After a second attempt was also frustrated by heavy fire, the battalion returned to Romagny.

On the afternoon of August 8, Das Reich outposts began reporting the advance of American forces to the south of the St. Hilaire–Mortain road. This was the newly committed 35th Division. This division had been part of Middleton's XX Corps moving past Avranches over the past few days. Due to the Mortain counter-attack, it was re-directed eastward to cover the gap between Mortain and Barenton on the 30th Division's right flank. It had

A rifle squad of Co. A, 1/119th Infantry race along the base of a hedgerow during the fighting near Romagny on August 9.

begun to advance northwestward out of St. Hilaire with the 134th Infantry on the left and the 137th Infantry on the right on the afternoon of August 7. By the late afternoon of August 8, it was southwest of Romagny and approaching the defensive perimeter of Das Reich.

Baum decided to stage a spoiling attack in the early evening, using 6. Kompanie, SS-Pz.Rgt. 2 from Das Reich led by Obersturmführer Willy Durr. The 134th Infantry was advancing through the fields south of the St. Hilaire–Mortain road, and the German column advanced past the rifle companies of 2/134th Infantry into the battalion's rear area. The 1st Platoon, Co. A, 737th Tank Battalion was parked near the 2nd Battalion command post when the German tanks made a surprise attack from the road. Four M4 tanks were quickly knocked out. Another German tank platoon hit the 134th Cannon Company, which fired their 105mm howitzer against the tanks to little effect before being overrun. A pair of M10 3in. GMC of A/654th Tank Destroyer Battalion intervened, losing two M10s. The surprise attack also overwhelmed the battalion motor park and aid station. Headquarters and rear area troops began to take the tanks under fire with bazookas. The raid ended after dark when the Panzers withdrew back toward Romagny.

The reinforcement that Hausser had promised to the Das Reich was the 10. SS-Panzer-Division "Frundsberg." This division was assigned to the scheme to renew the offensive toward Avranches sometime around August 11. The divisional commander, Brigadeführer Heinz Harmel, had been briefed that the staging area at Barenton was being held by the 275. Infanterie-Division. In fact, the 275. Infanterie-Division had been largely destroyed in the previous fighting. Its Kampfgruppe Schlee, consisting of about 150 stragglers, had been in Barenton until August 7 when they were pushed out by the southernmost element of the 30th Division, the 3/120th Infantry. US forces in Barenton expanded with the arrival of a substantial portion of the 2nd Armored Division, which had been ordered to the Barenton–Domfront area that day. The Frundsberg sent its reconnaissance battalion down the Ger–Barenton road, only to quickly discover that the US Army was firmly in control of Barenton. Instead of deploying around Barenton, the Frundsberg began taking up defensive positions in Ger, the main road junction east of Mortain. The 2nd Armored Division began advancing up the Barenton–Ger road on August 8, blocking the planned advance route for the Frundsberg.

A squad from Co. A, 1/119th Infantry moves through the *bocage* near Romagny during the fighting there on August 9. The GI in the center is armed with a 2.36in. bazooka rocket launcher and M1 carbine.

NORTH OF MORTAIN

The change in command of the 116. Panzer-Division led to a change in tactics, with Pz.Gren. Rgt. 60 attempting to infiltrate the positions of Lt. Col. Van Bond's 39th Infantry near Chérencé-le-Roussel. Two companies managed to secure the hamlet of La Grand

Mardelle, located about a kilometer north of Chérencé. Bond sought support from the neighboring 4th Division and was provided with a company from 1/8th Infantry to clear out La Grande Mardelle. The infantry was supported by a platoon of M4 tanks from the C/746th Tank Battalion. Lacking anti-tank weapons, the Panzergrenadiers were overwhelmed by the attack, and 86 prisoners were taken from I./Pz.Gren.Rgt. 60 in the attack. This ended the daylight attacks, but Pz.Gren.Rgt. 60 tried another attack in the early morning hours of August 9 accompanied by a few PzKpw IV tanks. American field artillery broke up the first two attacks, but they resumed again around 0700hrs. This attack was beaten back by artillery, and for good measure a sortie of a dozen P-47s conducted a dive-bombing attack. The 39th Infantry tried to regain the initiative by pushing the 2/39th Infantry eastward to cut the Sourdeval–St. Pois road. This advance was short lived once it encountered a German strongpoint near Mont Furgon supported by tanks. Panzergrenadier-Regiment 60 counter-attacked the 2/39th Infantry, but once again was beaten off with the support of artillery.

The most intense fighting on Tuesday, August 8 occurred in the northern sector of the battle, largely due to aggressive actions by Col. Boudinot's CCB, 3rd Armored Division and the 4th Infantry Division. Combat Command B had three task forces in operation that day, Team 1 under Col. Dorrance Roysdon pushing out of Le Mesnil-Adelée toward Le Mesnil-Tôve from the west, Team 2 from the Juvigny area toward Le Mesnil-Tôve from the south, and Team 3 on a separate reconnaissance mission toward Cuves to the north. The attack toward Le Mesnil-Tôve was supported by 3/119th Infantry, 30th Division. At the same time, the 8th Infantry, 4th Division was pushing on Le Mesnil-Tôve from the northwest.

Le Mesnil-Tôve had become a defensive hub for Kampfgruppe Schake after its retreat from Le Mesnil-Adelée the previous day. The Panther tank battalion of the 116. Panzer-Division, I./Pz.Rgt. 24, remained attached to Kampfgruppe Schake during this fighting, and took up defensive positions south of the village, blocking the approach routes of Team 1 and Team 2. Panzerjäger-Abteilung 38 was located closer to the village, oriented toward the southwest. Panzergrenadier-Regiment 304 was assigned to cover the approach routes to the north against the advancing 4th Division, but also had a battalion facing south to support the Panther tanks against CCB 3rd Armored Division.

The fighting on Tuesday, August 8 was costly on both sides. The terrain was farmland broken up by *bocage* that was well suited to defense. A later CCB report described the area as "not suitable for the employment of armor." Team 1 had already been attached to the 119th Infantry since the start of the operation, and during the course of the day, Team 2 was also put under 119th Infantry command. On August 8, Team 3 was attached to the 1/119th Infantry to take part in the fighting at L'Abbaye Blanche.

The various elements of the CCB 3rd Armored Division, 3/119th Infantry, and the two regiments of 4th Division gradually encircled Le Mesnil-Tôve on August 8 from all sides but the east. Panzergrenadier-Regiment 304 launched several counter-attacks against the US infantry, but was gradually forced back closer to the village. The most destructive aspect of the fighting was the heavy use of artillery by both sides.

On August 9, a major American counter-attack was in preparation to push eastward to create a more solid perimeter between the units assaulting

Le Mesnil-Tôve and the forces immediately south around St. Barthélemy. In the midst of a conference by the senior commanders, a German artillery barrage struck the area, killing the Team 2 leader, Col. William Cornog, and the 2/36th Armored Infantry commander, Col. Vincent Cockefair, and injuring several other officers. The other task force commander, Col. Roysdon, narrowly escaped the same fate during another artillery barrage. Kampfgruppe Schake also took heavy losses during the incessant artillery exchanges. This portion of the battle remained locked in stalemate for four days with the American infantry gradually grinding through the German defenses a hedgerow at a time.

Further south, much of the fighting on August 8–9 centered around a small road junction, called RJ 278 in American accounts, on the St. Barthélemy–Mortain road. The road junction was attacked on the morning of August 9 by 2/12th Infantry, 4th Division, without success after running into an assault by SS-Pz.Gren.Rgt. 1. Although the American attack was stopped, the 2/12th Infantry in turn halted the German attack. A similar attack by 1/12th Infantry was halted by the II./SS-Pz.Gren.Rgt. 4 further to the south.

Major-General Hobbs of the 30th Division decided to try a different approach. The 30th Division built up a composite force based around Lt. Col. Samuel Hogan's Task Force 3, 3rd Armored Division. This consisted mainly of a single tank battalion, the 3/33rd Armored. The attack began around noon on August 9 with riflemen of the 2/119th Infantry riding on Hogan's tanks. The approach path was from the south via the L'Abbaye Blanche area instead of the swamp area immediately to the west that had been used by 2/12th Infantry. Hogan's column was hit by German artillery, forcing the infantry to dismount. He decided to attack the road junction using only his tanks. However, the area had been heavily reinforced by II./SS-Pz.Gren.Rgt. 4 due to previous attacks, and Hogan lost nine M4 tanks to German tank and anti-tank gun fire in short order. The American tank column withdrew, and II./SS-Pz.Gren.Rgt. 4 attempted to prepare a counter-attack. However, Hogan had positioned a forward observer on a hill overlooking the road-junction and the German infantry was hit by 105mm fire from Hogan's M4 assault gun platoon.

A 57mm anti-tank gun of the 12th Infantry, 4th Division during the fighting for road junction RJ 278 on the St. Barthélemy–Mortain road on August 9.

Fighting flared up again in the late afternoon in a combined attack by 1/117th Infantry and 12th Infantry. The 1/117th Infantry tried to push back into St. Barthélemy, but the attack was disrupted when the battalion was nearly struck by a preparatory barrage, and then by a German artillery strike. The 12th Infantry attempted to advance over the road and secure RJ 278 using all three of its battalions, but it was frustrated again by intense German field artillery. During the fighting for RJ 278, US spotter aircraft identified 42 German artillery batteries. In contrast to the first day of the offensive when there were few German field artillery batteries deployed, over the course of August 8, 47. Panzer-Korps had managed to bring up and emplace both the divisional and corps artillery. Although the US field artillery attempted to dilute this with counter-battery fire, it was unsuccessful.

REINVIGORATING LÜTTICH

The fighting on August 7–9 ended in stalemate. The 30th Division was able to hold the German attack at bay but was unable to regain many objectives. Even with the aid of other VII Corps units, the 30th Division was still substantially outnumbered and outgunned by 47. Panzer-Korps.

The 47. Panzer-Korps attack became exhausted almost immediately on August 7 due to stubborn American resistance and the paralyzing effect of the air attacks. On Monday evening, August 7, Funck recommended that the 47. Panzer-Korps return to its start line. German efforts to break the stalemate on August 8–9 were half-hearted. This was in part due to the mixed messages coming from senior German commanders as well as the depleted state of many of the German units. Although there were exhortations from Berlin that the advance must continue, at the same time senior leaders had acknowledged that Operation *Lüttich* had failed on its first day and would have to be substantially reinforced in order to reach Avranches. On the one hand, units were encouraged to press forward in the hopes of securing new inroads into the

American defenses. At the same time, Kluge tolerated the practice of restricting major attacks to hours of darkness or fog to limit the vulnerability of the attack force to Allied power. Attrition of the Panzer force had to be avoided to keep the 47. Panzer-Korps strong enough for a second push to Avranches. Plans to reinforce the attack with the 9. Panzer-Division were frustrated by the attacks of VII Corps around Mayenne south of the Mortain sector, which forced its commitment there to reinforce the 708. Infanterie-Division.

One of the first steps for an expanded offensive was the transfer of Gen. der Pz. Walter Krüger's 58. Panzer-Korps headquarters to take over control of the southern wing of the attack, starting with Das Reich on the morning of August 9. On the afternoon of August 9, Kluge ordered 11. Panzer-Division in southern France to begin moving toward Normandy via Blois and Chartres. In the event, this order was later countermanded by Hitler since evidence of an impending Allied amphibious landing in southern France was accumulating.

Hitler criticized Kluge's first Avranches attack, complaining that "The 47. Panzer-Korps attack was ordered too early, too weak and in weather that was favorable for the enemy air forces and therefore unsuccessful." Shaking off his torpor from earlier in the month, on Monday afternoon, August 7, Hitler laid out his concepts for a renewed Avranches offensive. These orders did not arrive at Kluge's forward command posts until 2000hrs that evening.

> The decision in the Battle of France depends on the attack on the southern wing of the 7. Armee. A unique opportunity, which will never return, had been given to OB West to drive into an extremely vulnerable enemy sector and thereby decisively change the situation. Therefore I command:
> 1. The attack will be conducted to the sea with daring and boldness.
> 2. Regardless of the risk, II. SS-Panzer-Korps and either 12. SS-Panzer-Division or 21. Panzer-Division will follow the first and second waves as a third wave to the attack.
> 3. The rear echelons of the attack will veer northward in order to collapse the Normandy front by a thrust into the deep flank and rear of the enemy facing the 7. Armee.
> 4. Existing gains will be expanded and exploited by attacking with the neighboring infantry divisions.
> 5. The greatest daring, determination and imagination must inspire all echelons of command. Each and every man must believe in victory. Cleaning up the rear areas and Brittany can wait until later.

Later in the day, Hitler met with the new Paris commander, Dietrich von Choltitz, whom he told that the Avranches attack would "throw the enemy into the sea." The third wave of Panzer divisions added to *Lüttich* was supposed to consist of the 9. SS-Panzer-Division and 10. SS-Panzer-Division from II. Panzer-Korps, plus either 12. SS-Panzer-Division or 21. Panzer-Division. In the event, only the 10. SS-Panzer-Division was ever committed to the Avranches force. Even before Operation *Lüttich* began, Hitler insisted that Kluge replace Funck with Eberbach, commander of Panzergruppe West.

Eberbach's command had undergone continual change in early August, first being renamed as Panzer-Armee West, then finally as 5. Panzer-Armee on August 7. Eberbach was instructed to form a new headquarters

The Encirclement Threat, August 7–11, 1944

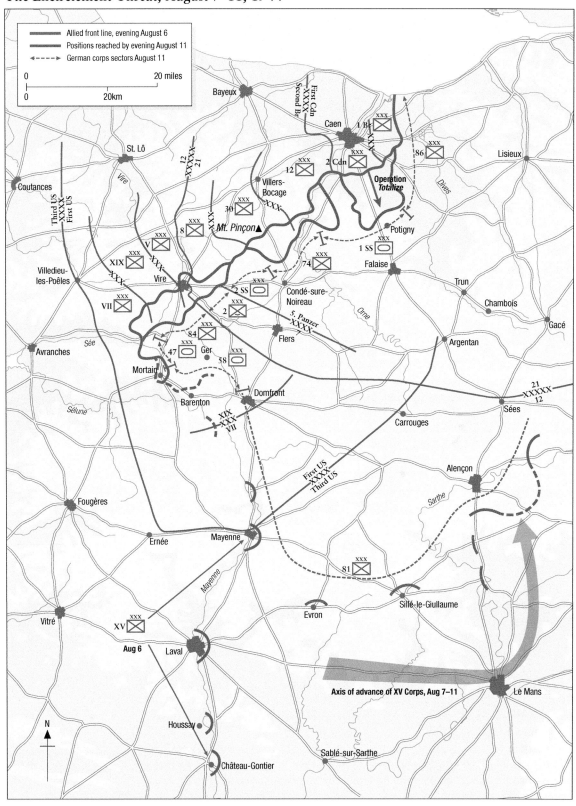

Allied front line, evening August 6
Positions reached by evening August 11
German corps sectors August 11

0   20 miles
0   20km

Bayeux

First Cdn
Second Br

Caen — 1 Br XXX

St. Lô   12 / 21 XXXX   2 Cdn XXX   86 XXX   Lisieux

Coutances   12 XXX   Operation *Totalize*

Vire

Villers-Bocage   30 XXX XXX

Third US / First US   8 XXX   Mt. Pinçon▲

Potigny

1 SS

Villedieu-les-Poêles   V XXX XXX   74 XXX   Falaise

XIX XXX XXX   Vire   Trun

VII XXX   2 SS XXX   Condé-sure-Noireau   Chambois

2 XXX   5. Panzer XXXX   Gacé

84 XXX   Flers   Argentan

Sée

47   Ger   58 XXX

Avranches

Mortain

Barenton   Domfront   21 XXXXX 12   Sées

Sélune   XIX XXX VII   Carrouges

First US XXXX Third US   Alençon

Fougères   Sarthe

Ernée   Mayenne   81 XXX

Mayenne

Vitré   XV XXX   Sillé-le-Giullaume

Evron

Aug 6   Laval

N

Houssay

Sablé-sur-Sarthe

Château-Gontier

Axis of advance of XV Corps, Aug 7–11   Le Mans

dubbed Angriffsgruppe Eberbach (Attack Group Eberbach) and later as Panzergruppe Eberbach. At the same time, Sepp Dietrich, commander of I. SS-Panzer-Korps, was instructed to take over the shriveled remnants of 5. Panzer-Armee on August 10. By August 9, 5. Panzer-Armee had been reduced to only three panzer divisions, 21. Panzer-Division, 9. SS-Panzer-Division, and 21. Panzer-Division, equipped with a paltry 54 tanks and 18 assault guns and tank destroyers.

Kluge was dismayed by Hitler's August 7 orders, realizing that they would strip the Caen front of its best divisions. Eberbach remarked in a telephone exchange with Kluge that "Failure of this [Avranches] attack could lead to the collapse of the entire Normandy front, but the order is so unequivocal that it must be obeyed." The second stage of Operation *Lüttich* originally was scheduled to start at 2200hrs on August 9. Although instructions were sent out to begin moving the additional Panzer divisions westward, other events completely undermined the scheme for the second Avranches attack.

On the night of August 7–8, the Canadian First Army launched Operation *Totalize*, aimed at Falaise. During the course of August 8, the Canadian attack built up such momentum that it threatened to break through the German defenses south of Caen. Kluge was forced to divert the 12. SS-Panzer-Division back to this sector, take away the Panther battalion of the newly arrived 9. Panzer-Division from the Avranches force, and leave the 9. SS-Panzer-Division in the Caen sector.

The Canadian drive on Falaise forced Hitler to recognize that the second *Lüttich* attack would have to be postponed until August 11 at the earliest. Nevertheless, he issued a second set of orders to Kluge on August 9, further detailing his plans for the Avranches attack. To avoid interference by Allied air power, Hitler noted the need to attack on an overcast day, or to conduct the attack during the night under conditions of a full moon.

Both Kluge and Eberbach were extremely pessimistic about the prospects for such an attack. Eberbach's force of nearly seven Panzer divisions could only muster 77 PzKpfw IV and 47 Panther tanks, even after Hitler had allotted them all of the theater reserve. This was only about half the size of the original Avranches force on August 7. Attrition during the first phase of *Lüttich* had been high. Fifty tanks, including 34 Panthers and 16 PzKpfw IVs, had been destroyed as well as 14 assault guns and tank destroyers. A large number of tanks and AFVs had suffered combat damage or mechanical problems and were no longer operational. German meteorologists forecast that the high-pressure front over France would not change until August 20, possibly bringing summer rain and clouds. However, the situation on the 7. Armee front facing the Americans was unraveling so quickly that these plans became entirely fanciful.

BRADLEY'S ENCIRCLEMENT PLAN

By Tuesday, August 8, Omar Bradley was convinced that VII Corps could hold at Mortain. From the Ultra decrypts, Bradley concluded that the Germans had thrown their last reserves into an ill-conceived attack that left the Wehrmacht in Normandy vulnerable to encirclement and destruction. Eisenhower was visiting Bradley's headquarters that day, and Bradley proposed that the 12th Army Group re-orient its offensive axis from eastward toward the Seine to northward toward Argentan. In combination with Montgomery's 21st Army Group, this would create the jaws of a vice that would trap the Germans west of the Seine River. In a telephone conference with Montgomery, the senior Allied commanders agreed to this course of action.

The prospects for the encirclement were largely contingent on the conduct of the Mortain battle and the eastward advance of Haislip's XV Corps. Haislip's force was the first portion of Patton's Third US Army that had been freed from the Brittany mission on August 6 and sent eastward. Operating against no significant German opposition, its advance had been rapid, capturing the city of Le Mans, deep in the German rear, on August 8. At the time, it consisted of only the 79th and 90th Infantry Divisions and the 5th Armored Division. Patton added the French 2e Division Blindée (Armored Division) to give it additional mobile strength, and that unit entered the corps zone on August 9. After erecting tactical bridging over the Sarthe River on August 9, XV Corps began heading north on August 10. Its short-term objective was the city of Alençon.

Hausser's 7. Armee had only the 81. Armee-Korps in the area, plus a variety of skeleton divisions such as the Panzer-Lehr-Division and 353. Infanterie-Division that had been largely destroyed in previous fighting. On August 10, XV Corps advanced halfway to Alençon, about 15 miles (24km). The northward change in direction of XV Corps was quickly recognized by 7. Armee and hasty steps were taken to reinforce the defenses in this area. Kampfgruppe Reich, based on Pz.Gren.Rgt. 10 of the 9. Panzer-Division under Oberstleutnant Johann Reich, was assigned to defend Alençon. The Panzer-Lehr-Division was also added to this defense, but a report that day grimly noted that it had only 150 riflemen in Pz.Gren.Rgt. 901, nine tanks and only six field guns. Late in the day, 49. Infanterie-Division was ordered to begin movement to Argentan to reinforce this sector. On August 10, 7. Armee captured some US Army documents that made it clear that the objective of XV Corps was Alençon.

The advance on Alençon created a crisis for Kluge's OB West. Aside from Paris itself, Alençon was the main German administrative and supply center for Normandy. Nevertheless, Hitler remained undecided whether to continue the attack toward Avranches or to deal with the unfolding disaster approaching Alençon.

THE RELIEF OF HILL 314

After three days of fighting around Mortain, the fighting around the town settled into a belligerent stalemate. Both sides continued local attacks, but the frontlines shifted very little. The main exception was on the southern approaches to Mortain, where the 35th Division had been given the task of reaching Mortain and relieving the "lost battalion" on Hill 314.

The most immediate problem for the 2/120th Infantry was the desperate need for supplies. The unit was running out of food, medical supplies, and ammunition. Most important was the need for fresh dry-cell batteries for the radios of the forward artillery observer teams. The VII Corps artillery was the main factor in shielding the 2/120th Infantry from the continual Das Reich attacks. Around 1625hrs, August 10, a flight of 12 C-47 transport aircraft with fighter escort flew about 300ft over Hill 314 to drop supplies. German small arms detonated one of the para-packs full of ammunition, but the

remaining 70 packs were released without issue. However, only about half of the packs were collected by the 2/120th Infantry, the remainder falling into German hands. The packs arriving in the E/120th Infantry area contained mainly food and ammunition but lacked medical supplies and batteries. It would take at least a day to organize another supply drop. In the meantime, Lt. Col. Lewis Vieman, commander of the 230th Field Artillery Battalion, proposed an emergency solution of shooting batteries and plasma into the 2/120th Infantry perimeter using empty artillery smoke projectiles. A first attempt using this unorthodox delivery method was attempted at 2145hrs that night, but darkness prevented collection of any of the parcels. Another attempt was made at first light on August 11.

When instructed by VII Corps on August 10 to relieve Hill 314, Maj. Gen. Paul Baade decided to use the 35th Division's reserve, Maj. William Gillis' 1/320th Infantry, reinforced with the attached 737th Tank Battalion. The attack by Task Force Gillis was scheduled for 1500hrs on August 10. The attack ran into immediate problems since Das Reich had anticipated an advance along this route as there were few roads through the *bocage*. Anti-tank guns were deployed in the hedgerows along the roads, supported by machine-gun nests. The first M4 tank of C/737th Tank Battalion was knocked out by an anti-tank gun, which was in turn knocked out by the following tank. The German infantry then unleashed machine-gun fire against the tanks, causing the tank-riding infantry of B/320th Infantry to hastily jump off. The 1/320th Infantry made slow progress against the German hedgerow defenses, finally pushing through a line held by the SS-Panzeraufklarung-Abt. 2. The battalion commander, Sturmbannführer Ernst Krag attempted to staunch the breach by shifting three more 7.5cm PaK 40 anti-tank guns to cover the road. The anti-tank guns knocked out the leading two tanks, and a fire-fight broke out between the infantry forces on both sides. Company C, 737th Tank Battalion decided to try to move cross-country through the *bocage* using hedgerow cutters welded to the bow of their tanks for Operation *Cobra*. These proved ineffective in breaching the hedgerows. Captain George Zurman, the company commander, was

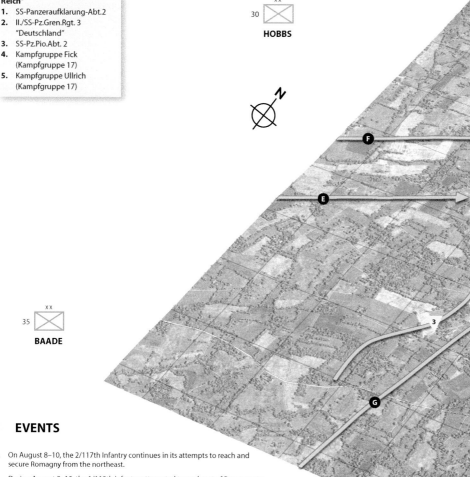

GERMAN FORCES
2. SS-Panzer-Division "Das Reich"
1. SS-Panzeraufklarung-Abt. 2
2. II./SS-Pz.Gren.Rgt. 3 "Deutschland"
3. SS-Pz.Pio.Abt. 2
4. Kampfgruppe Fick (Kampfgruppe 17)
5. Kampfgruppe Ullrich (Kampfgruppe 17)

30 ⊠ XX
HOBBS

ROMA

35 ⊠ XX
BAADE

EVENTS

1. On August 8–10, the 2/117th Infantry continues in its attempts to reach and secure Romagny from the northeast.

2. During August 8–10, the 1/119th Infantry attempted to push out of Romagny to the northeast to relieve the 2/120th Infantry trapped on Hill 314 but is stopped by tank gun fire from the Das Reich perimeter located southwest of Mortain.

3. On August 10, VII Corps instructs Maj. Gen. Paul Baade, commander of the 35th Division, to relieve the trapped 2/120th Infantry on Hill 314. He assembles Task Force Gillis consisting of Maj. William Gillis' 1/320th Infantry, reinforced with the attached 737th Tank Battalion. The attack by Task Force Gillis is scheduled for 1500hrs on August 10. The attack runs into immediate problems since Das Reich had anticipated an advance along this route and has positioned anti-tank guns in the *bocage* along the roads.

4. As Task Force Gillis advances directly toward Hill 314, the neighboring 3/137 Infantry and 2/134th Infantry spearhead the regimental advances further east, dislodging German defenses along the Bion–Mortain road.

5. The 1/320th Infantry makes slow but steady progress through the German hedgerow defenses, finally pushing through a line held by the SS-Panzeraufklarung-Abt. 2. The battalion commander, Sturmbannführer Ernst Krag attempts to staunch the breach by shifting three 7.5cm PaK 40 anti-tank guns to cover the road.

6. Company C, 737th Tank Battalion takes such heavy losses in the advance that it withdraws and is replaced by Co. A. On reaching the Mortain–Bion road, the commander of Co. A, 737th Tank Battalion insisted that the tanks return to the rear for refueling and rearming, much to the chagrin of the accompanying infantry.

7. Three M4 tanks of Co. C, 737th Tank Battalion have become separated from the rest of the company and reach the base of Hill 314. On hearing the firing from the rest of the relief column to the south, the three tanks under withdraw back to the south. With nightfall approaching, 1/320th Infantry take up a defensive position in a hedgerow-lined field near the hamlet of Clairet.

8. Around 0100hrs in the predawn hours of August 11, Das Reich stages a counter-attack including tanks to overwhelm the 1/320th Infantry but the attack is halted. The Das Reich force is strengthened and a much larger attack begins at 0700hrs. The Co. B defenses collapse under the attack, forcing the 1/320th Infantry to withdraw about 300 yards south. The German attack runs out of energy when it encounters a fresh company of the 320th Infantry that has been moving forward since dawn to reinforce Task Force Gillis.

9. On August 11, Company A, 119th Infantry has finally secured the village of Romagny with tank support that afternoon.

10. The attack on 1/320th Infantry has stripped many of the Das Reich strongpoints further east that have been opposing the two other regiments of the 35th Division. The 3/137th Infantry reaches Bion on August 11, occupied by Krag's SS-Pz.Aufklarungs-Abt.2. Das Reich is unwilling to lose the village of Bion or control of the road, and so launches another infantry attack with tank support. The village of Bion is flattened by a US artillery barrage and the advance along the Bion–Mortain road turns into a bloody stalemate for the rest of the day.

11. The 30th Division secures control of Romagny and Hill 285 on August 11. At 1800hrs, SS-Pz.Gren.Rgt. 3 is ordered to withdraw back to a new defense line closer to Mortain, a process that begins after dark.

12. The German retreat from the Mortain area starts after dark on the night of August 11, and continues after dawn on the morning of August 12.

13. Around 0820hrs on the morning of Saturday, August 12, the 320th Infantry, 35th Division finally reach the encircled forces of the 2/120th Infantry on Hill 314.

THE RELIEF OF THE "LOST BATTALION" ON HILL 314, AUGUST 10–12

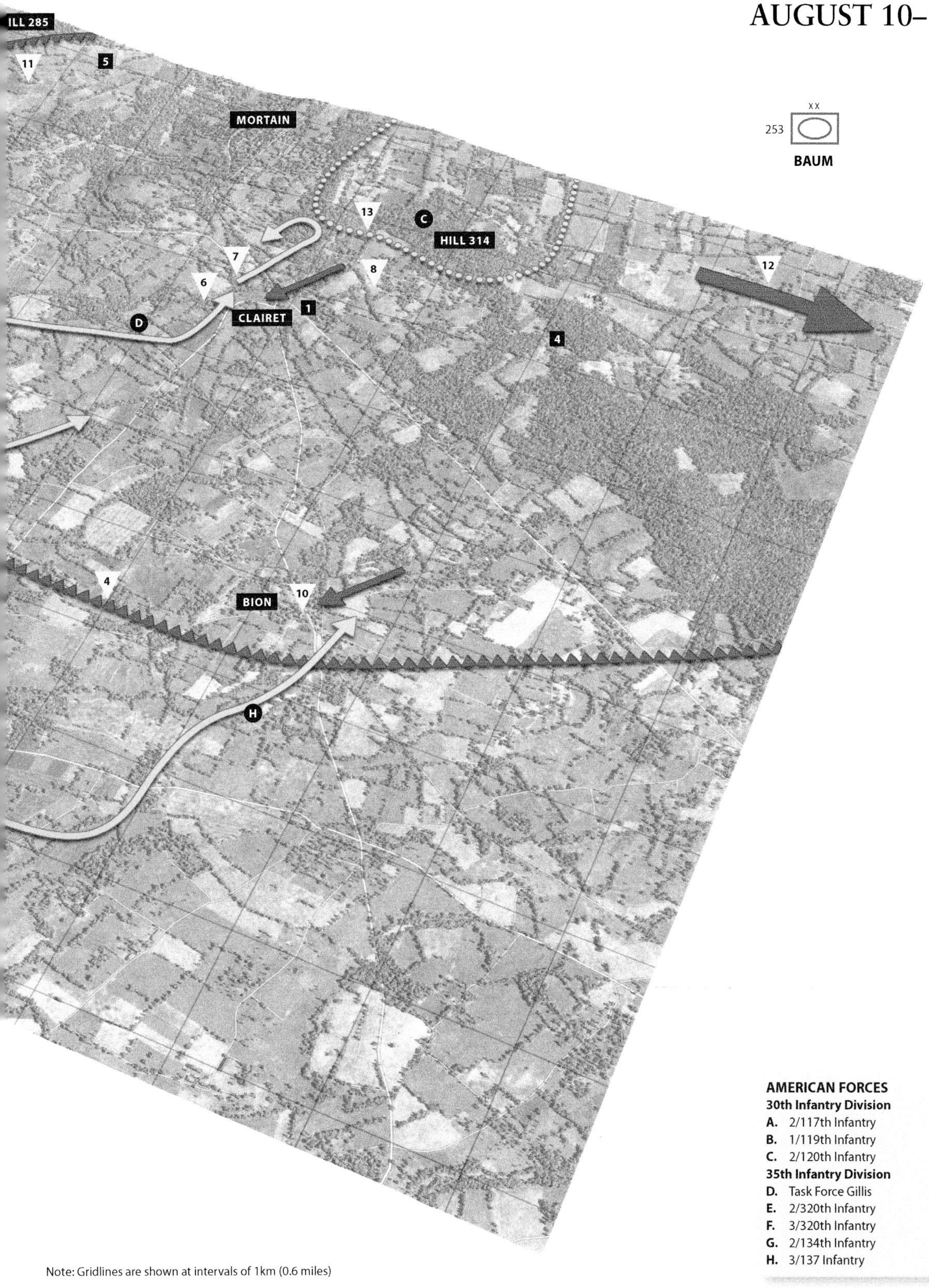

ILL 285

11

5

MORTAIN

13

C

HILL 314

7

8

6

12

D

CLAIRET

1

4

4

BION

10

H

253 | XX
BAUM

AMERICAN FORCES
30th Infantry Division
A. 2/117th Infantry
B. 1/119th Infantry
C. 2/120th Infantry
35th Infantry Division
D. Task Force Gillis
E. 2/320th Infantry
F. 3/320th Infantry
G. 2/134th Infantry
H. 3/137 Infantry

Note: Gridlines are shown at intervals of 1km (0.6 miles)

These five soldiers from Co. H, 2/120th Infantry were among the survivors of the battles for Hill 314 and are seen here on August 15 discussing plans. In the center is the platoon commander, Lt. Robert Warnick.

injured when his tank overturned on its side having tried to plow through a hedgerow. Due to the heavy losses in Co. C, the neighboring Co. A, 737th Tank Battalion took the lead with a platoon of infantry from B/320th Infantry. Several more tanks were lost to fire from German anti-tank guns and a PzKpfw IV tank protecting Krag's battalion headquarters.

After reaching the Mortain–Bion road, Capt. Martin Conde of Co. A, 737th Tank Battalion insisted that the tanks return to the rear for refueling and rearming, much to the chagrin of the accompanying infantry. The 1/320th Infantry continued its advance to Hill 314 without tank support. Curiously enough, three M4 tanks of Co. C, 737th Tank Battalion had become separated from the rest of the company and had reached the base of Hill 314. On hearing the firing from the rest of the relief column to the south, the three tanks under Lt. Samuel Belk decided to withdraw back to the south and join Task Force Gillis. In the process, Belk's tank was knocked out by an anti-tank gun. With nightfall approaching, 1/320th Infantry took up a defensive position in a hedgerow-lined field near the hamlet of Clairet.

The advance by 1/320th Infantry from the south was aided by other fighting around Mortain on August 11. Company A, 119th Infantry had finally secured the village of Romagny with tank support that afternoon, to the immediate northwest of Task Force Gillis. That night, the two divisional commanders, Hobbs and Baade, met to discuss coordination of the push the following day.

The advance by Task Force Gillis threatened the Das Reich defenses on the southern side of Mortain, potentially cutting off the best eastward escape routes. A small counter-attack including tanks attempted to overwhelm the 1/320th Infantry around 0100hrs in the predawn hours of August 11, but was halted. The counter-attack force was strengthened and conducted a much larger attack at 0700hrs. The Company B defenses collapsed under the dawn attack, forcing the 1/320th Infantry to withdraw about 300 yards south.

The German attack ran out of energy when it encountered another infantry battalion that had been moving forward since dawn to reinforce Task Force Gillis. Elements of the 1/320th Infantry remained isolated for much of the day and subjected to local Das Reich attacks. Isolated and exhausted, the battalion began to fall back until runners arrived indicating that 3/320th Infantry would arrive and take the lead in the advance on Hill 134.

The Das Reich strongpoints further east were engaged by the two other regiments of the 35th Division. The 3/137th Infantry reached Bion, occupied by Krag's SS-Pz.Aufklarungs-Abt. 2, and by later in the morning, the 35th Division was moving three rifle battalions northward along the main Mortain–Barenton road. Das Reich was unwilling to lose the village of Bion or control of the road, and so launched another infantry attack with tank support. The village of Bion was flattened by a US artillery barrage and the advance along the Bion–Mortain road turned into a bloody stalemate for the rest of the day.

The gradual erosion of the southern Das Reich defenses was repeated in other sectors on August 11, with the 30th Division securing control of Romagny and Hill 285. However, it was developments further afield that would cause dramatic changes on the Mortain front on Saturday, August 12. Unbeknownst to the 30th Infantry Division, Berlin had decided to withdraw from the Mortain front for reasons explained in more detail below. The night of August 11–12 was unusually active due to heavy German artillery barrages along the front. To some of the more perceptive American officers, it seemed as though the Germans were expending their remaining reserves of artillery ammunition. The Americans responded with their first heavy bombardment of the town of Mortain that night, causing extensive damage.

The German retreat from the Mortain area started after dark on the night of August 11, and continued after dawn on the morning of August 12. One column passed close enough to Hill 314 that Lt. Weiss, the forward

Panzergruppe Eberbach vs. XV Corps, August 9–12

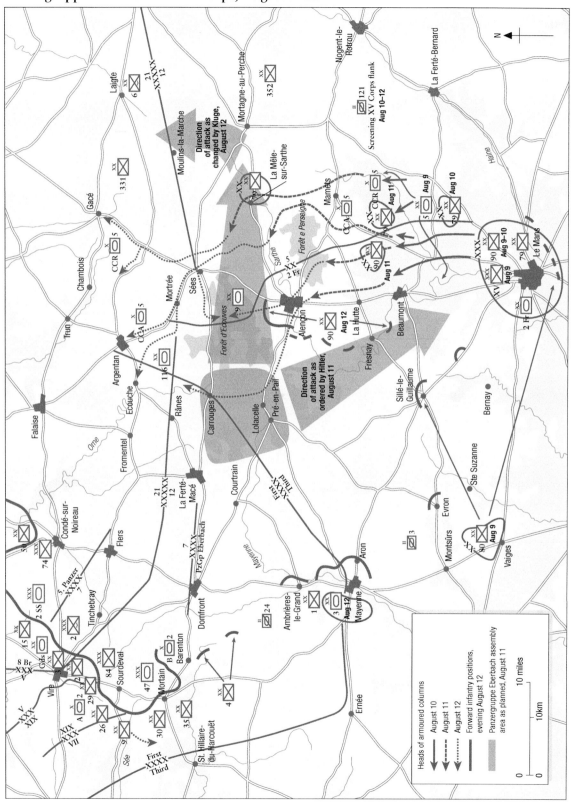

The town of Mortain was badly damaged by intense US artillery fire on the night of August 11/12, shortly before the German evacuation.

observer for the 230th Field Artillery Battalion, called in an artillery strike. It was later estimated that about 50–100 vehicles were knocked out in this final barrage.

Around 0820hrs on the morning of Saturday, August 12, the 320th Infantry, 35th Division finally reached the encircled forces of the 2/120th Infantry on Hill 314. By the time they were relieved, the force on Hill 314 had been reduced to 370 men of the roughly 700 men on the hill on the first day of the battle. Casualties in the 2/120th Battalion were 277 men killed, captured, or missing. Casualties in the 30th Division as a whole during the six days of fighting was about 1,800 men killed, wounded, and missing.

There are no accurate figures for German casualties during the battle for Mortain. The hospital in Mortain housed about 2,000 German wounded prior to the evacuation. French civilian casualties are not precisely known. About 800 civilians took advantage of the tunnels in the Cabremont mine for shelter during the conduct of the battle. This was about half of the pre-war population of the town.

REORIENTING LÜTTICH

German commanders in France had been skeptical about the scheme to stage a second attack toward Avranches. The heavy casualties suffered in the initial attack on August 7, and the inability of Heeresgruppe B to provide sufficient reinforcements for an enlarged attack, suggested that a renewed offensive to Avranches had no prospects for success. The plans were kept alive only by Hitler's manic insistence that a second *Lüttich* offensive could have a decisive impact on reversing the catastrophe facing the Wehrmacht in France.

Dietrich's 5. Panzer-Armee had managed to stop the Canadians' Operation *Totalize*, but this offensive on August 8–9 had pushed Montgomery's 21st Army Group nearer to the crossroads town of Falaise. While the Canadians

Following the withdrawal of 47. Panzer-Korps from the Mortain area, the 28th Infantry Division conducted the pursuit toward the German staging areas around Sourdeval and Ger. This is a column of the 28th Division on August 13, 1944.

had faced stiff resistance, Patton's Third US Army was racing through the rear areas of the Wehrmacht in northern France, where there were only hasty defenses at best.

To all but the blind, it was obvious that the Allies were on the verge of trapping the Wehrmacht in a sack. Many of the Wehrmacht's best units in France were tied down in the stalemate in the Mortain area. The *Lüttich* attack force was about 50 miles (75km) from Falaise and Argentan and so could contribute nothing to repulsing the British and American attacks that threatened to close the Normandy trap.

In the pre-dawn hours of August 11, Kluge held a telephone conference with Eberbach about the possibilities for the renewal of Operation *Lüttich*. Eberbach estimated that the attack could begin no sooner than August 20 in order to permit sufficient strength to be assembled and to wait for inclement weather to ward off the Allied air threat. In the afternoon, Kluge held a conference with Eberbach and Hausser. By this time, the situation around Alençon was more clearly understood. All three senior commanders agreed that for the time being, there was no chance of launching another attack toward Avranches. Their immediate concern was to crush the American XV Corps attack toward Alençon–Argentan before it could join Montgomery's 21st Army Group, thereby trapping Heeresgruppe B. At 1300hrs, an alert was sent to 47. Panzer-Korps as a preliminary warning to prepare for withdrawal to the Alençon–Argentan sector after dark on the night of August 11–12. Krüger's 58. Panzer-Korps would manage the Mortain sector after the withdrawal. Panzergruppe Eberbach, headquartered near Alençon, would direct the attacks against XV Corps. Due to the urgency of the situation, the 116. Panzer-Division was the first unit to be pulled out of the Mortain sector on the afternoon of August 11. It began moving toward Alençon in the daylight that afternoon in spite of the risk of air attack.

After the conference concluded, Kluge telephoned Jodl at OKW headquarters by phone and discussed the emergency situation. Kluge recommended pulling back the entire 7. Armee to more defensible positions, and he explained his plans for the counter-attack against XV Corps. A change of this magnitude would require Hitler's permission. In the meantime, the

Two GIs from the 110th Infantry, 28th Division guard German prisoners captured in Lonlay l'Abbaye on August 16, 1944. This village had been a staging area for the 116. Panzer-Division for Operation *Lüttich*.

Panzer division commanders were issued an alert order to withdraw from Mortain under the cover of darkness at 2100hrs on August 11. Efforts were made to keep this movement secret by conducting vigorous and noisy artillery barrages along the Mortain front to mask the sounds of the movement.

Hitler approved of Kluge's plan around midnight on August 11–12 with a new set of instructions: "The serious threat to the deep southern flank of Heeresgruppe B requires that this danger be eliminated by an offensive… The American XV Corps in the area of Le Mans–Mamers–Alençon will be defeated in a concentric attack. One Panzer corps will hit the enemy force that is attacking in the direction of Alençon and Mamers in its deep flank… In order to disengage the Panzer corps for this attack, forces within 7. Armee must be displaced. I concur in a minor withdrawal between Sourdeval and Mortain in order to release these forces…"

In reality, Kluge had waited too late to create an effective counter-attack against XV Corps. Although the 47. Panzer-Korps did disengage without major incident, it could not move quickly enough to respond to XV Corps. Beyond this, 47. Panzer-Korps had become exhausted in the Mortain fighting, suffering heavy losses in men and machines. A report on its supply situation at the end of August 10 noted that "supply of fuel and main types of ammunition already strained and in regards to future intentions, not assured."

On August 11, Eberbach reached Alençon and found the city defenses to be a shambles. The German administrative organization was in total chaos, expecting the arrival of American tank columns at any moment. Eberbach attempted to buy time by using the forces at hand to slow the American advance. Instead of establishing his headquarters in the city, he moved it into the neighboring countryside. The battered 9. Panzer-Division was assigned the defense of the Forêt d'Ecouves, south of the Carrouges–Sées highway, while the 116. Panzer-Division would shield Argentan along the Carrouges–Argentan highway.

The 116. Panzer-Division was on the road by the late afternoon of August 11. The attempt to replace the troublesome Schwerin added to the chaos. Walter Reinhardt from Funck's staff served as the interim commander until the arrival of Oberst Georg von der Marwitz, but Marwitz was killed after his command car was strafed on August 10. Oberst Gerhard Müller was appointed next. Müller was an experienced Panzer leader, commanding Panzer-Regiment 5 at El Alamein and most recently leading the 12. Panzer-Division on the Russian Front. However, he only arrived on August 11 as the division was making its mad dash for Alençon, all the while under Allied air attack.

The 116. Panzer-Division departed the Mortain sector on August 10 in two columns, the northern column with most of its tank strength along the northern route via Flers to Argentan, and the second column with the divisions' administrative elements and one Panzergrenadier regiment via Domfront to Sées.

The plan was for the 116. Panzer-Division to conduct a coordinated defense of Argentan with 9. Panzer-Division, already in the area. This plan went awry from the start due to the rapid pace of the American advance. Haislip's XV

Corps raced through Mamers, 15 miles (25km) southeast of Alençon on August 11, and skirted around the Forêt de Perseigne due to inaccurate reports that it contained two full-strength German divisions. Haislip instructed the 5th Armored Division to avoid the congestion of Alençon, and aim instead for Sées, located 13 miles (20km) northwest of Alençon.

The 116. Panzer-Division reached the Alençon area on Saturday, August 12 and began deploying from the march without any information on the location of enemy forces. Without having the time to consolidate its scattered units, the division was demolished in piecemeal fashion. Disregarding the instructions from XV Corps, Gén. de div. Jacques Leclerc, commander of the 2e Division Blindée, deployed his three combat commands to clean out the Forêt d'Ecouves, dislodging the battered 9. Panzer-Division.

The lead elements of the 116. Panzer-Division, Pz.Gen.Rgt. 156, attempted hasty attacks against the 5th Armored Division and 2e Division Blindée over the course of August 12, suffering heavy losses in the process. Much of the division's artillery was lost when the division's forward command post near Mortrée was overrun. The Panther tanks from I./Pz.Rgt. 24 became caught up in a series of skirmishes with US and French Sherman tanks in Mortrée and the Brousées woods. The tanks of Pz.Rgt. 16 along with some remnants of the Panzer-Lehr Division and 9. Panzer-Division were overrun by the 2e Division Blindée in the Francheville area. French and American forces claimed to have destroyed a hundred armored vehicles and taken 1,500 prisoners that day alone.

Although most of the 116. Panzer-Division was disrupted in the fighting on August 12, Pz.Gen.Rgt. 60 did manage to set up a defense line outside Argentan. Hauptmann. Karl Pfannkuche's Pz.Rgt. 33 from 9. Panzer-Division

The French 2e Division Blindée was first committed to combat with XV Corps on the approaches to Alençon. This is a M4A2 number 26 "Iseran" commanded by Maréchal de Logis Martin, and part of the 2e Peleton, 2e Escadron, 1er Regiment de Chasseurs d'Afrique. The embossed Somua plate on the front of the tank is a reminder that this unit originally served with the Free French forces in 1943 in Tunisia on Somua S.35 cavalry tanks. This particular tank took part in the fighting toward Argentan and was finally lost in combat on March 1, 1945.

The 116. Panzer-Division was the first element of Panzergruppe Eberbach to attempt to halt the XV Corps advance on Argentan. During fighting on August 12, it suffered heavy casualties, including this Panther number 413 of 4. Schwadron, I./Pz.Rgt. 24 in Mortrée during fighting with the 5th Armored Division. It is seen here being recovered by US troops.

arrived late in Argentan and was absorbed into the 116. Panzer-Division defenses. By the end of the day, any chance of an immediate German counter-attack against XV Corps had evaporated. The best that could be hoped for was the creation of a thin defense line. Over the course of Sunday, August 13, other units from the Mortain sector began arriving, including elements of the 1. SS-Panzer-Division and 2. Panzer-Division. By this date, these units were badly understrength. Eberbach estimated that the 1. SS-Panzer-Division was down to 30 tanks from about 105 at the start of the Mortain attack and the 2. Panzer-Division to about 25 from 60 tanks. The 9. Panzer-Division had lost virtually all of its tanks except for its Panther battalion in Argentan. The 2. Panzer-Division was deployed to the west of Argentan near Ecouché and the 1. SS-Panzer-Division from La Ferté-Macé through Carrouges.

In a telephone conversation with OB West headquarters that morning, Sepp Dietrich, head of 5. Panzer-Armee, recommended that the Wehrmacht in Normandy retreat immediately before it was encircled and destroyed. "If the front held by the 5. Panzer-Armee and 7. Armee is not withdrawn immediately and if every effort is not made to move the forces toward the east and out of the threatened encirclement, Heeresgruppe B will have to write off both armies. Within a very short time, resupplying the troops with ammunition and fuel will no longer be possible. Therefore, immediate measures are necessary to move to the east before such movement is definitely too late. Soon it will be possible for the enemy to fire into the pocket with artillery from all sides."

Operation *Totalize*, the Canadian First Army offensive to Falaise, was halted on Friday, August 11, short of its goal. Although it had pushed Montgomery's 21st Army Group ten miles (16km) further south, it was still nine miles (15km) to Falaise, and 22 miles (35km) to Argentan. Montgomery's directive on August 11 was for the Canadian First Army and the British Second Army to capture Falaise "as the first priority," after which First Canadian Army was to close the gap to the US Army by capturing Argentan. This effort began three days later on Monday, August 14 as Operation *Tractable*.

THE HALT ORDER CONTROVERSY

On the morning of Sunday, August 13, Haislip's XV Corps was instructed by Patton to "push slowly in the direction of Falaise and make contact with the British there." The 5th Armored Division was instructed to gain control of the roads leading east out of Argentan to prevent German troops escaping, while at the same time, it was instructed not to become involved in "a serious fight for the town." The 2e Division Blindée was instructed to disengage from the Forêt d'Ecouves and take up positions south of Argentan; the 90th Division was instructed to take over this sector. These orders changed on Sunday afternoon when Bradley's 12th Army Group headquarters instructed Patton and Haislip to halt the northward advance.

The XV Corps "halt order" was one of the most controversial decisions of the Normandy campaign, and widely blamed for the failure of the Allies to close the Falaise–Argentan Gap in a timely fashion before the escape of a large portion of the German forces. The actual reason for the halt order has been obscured for many decades due to the need to protect the Ultra signals intelligence secret.

Ultra decrypts provided the senior Allied commanders with a solid indication of German intentions during the critical days of Friday August 11 through Sunday August 13. The instructions to Panzergruppe Eberbach to prepare for movement to Alençon at 1300hrs on August 11 was intercepted and decoded hours later, and an emergency warning issued to Ultra recipients at 2128hrs that day. Another Ultra message on the afternoon of August 12 revealed the evacuation of 47. Panzer-Korps from the Mortain sector and the transfer of 116. Panzer-Division to the Alençon area. Several Luftwaffe messages provided instructions for air support of a forthcoming operation by Panzergruppe Eberbach. The most critical bit of information was relayed to Bradley's headquarters as an emergency message from Bletchley Park at

1030hrs on August 13, based on a Flivo message from Kluge's Heeresgruppe B headquarters that the withdrawal from Mortain to the Alençon area was being undertaken to build up forces to attack XV Corps. It was this message more than any other that led to Bradley's halt order to XV Corps a few hours later. This message indicated that the Germans were planning to use the Mortain attack force, but in a new direction, against the vulnerable left flank of Haislip's XV Corps.

What was particularly worrisome to Bradley was that the Panzergruppe Eberbach attack would strike into a gap between XV Corps' left flank and Collins' VII Corps of the First US Army. Besides ordering XV Corps to halt and take up defensive positions, Bradley instructed Collins' VII Corps to take advantage of the void on August 14 and to tighten up boundaries between his VII Corps and the exposed left flank of Haislip's XV Corps. The 3rd Armored Division was on the right flank of VII Corps and reached Rânes on August 14, where it saw heavy fighting after bumping into the vanguard of Panzergruppe Eberbach, 2. Panzer-Division, and 1. SS-Panzer-Division. This costly action helped fill the gap between VII Corps and XV Corps, though it by no means precluded a further German Panzer attack.

Bradley saw no reason to have XV Corps push any further toward Argentan over the following few days, due to the lingering threat from Panzergruppe Eberbach. At 1000hrs on Tuesday, August 15, Bletchley Park transmitted a signal sent at 1605hrs on Monday afternoon, August 14 indicating that two *Kampfgruppen* of the 2. SS-Panzer-Division would arrive north of Argentan that night and that the 2. Panzer-Division would attack and capture Ecouché that day. This threat convinced Bradley to leave most of XV Corps in a defensive posture for the time being.

Once the Argentan front had stabilized, on August 15, Bradley allowed Patton to begin committing elements of XV Corps to the advance on the Seine River, starting with the 5th Armored Division. Here, an M4 medium tank of the 5th Armored Division is seen passing an abandoned 7.5cm PaK 40 anti-tank gun on the smoke-filled streets of Dreux, their first objective.

Bradley did allow Patton to dispatch the 5th Armored Division eastward toward Dreux. This was the first stage of Patton's effort to take advantage of the chaos in Heeresgruppe B and begin the race to the Seine, leading to a deep envelopment of the German army in northern France over the course of the next week.

The role of Ultra in prompting Bradley's halt order to XV Corps on August 13 may be obvious now since the declassification of the Ultra secret. But the real reasons for the decision were obscured for decades due to the sensitivity of the Ultra decryption program. Most of the memoirs and official histories of this campaign were written before the declassification of Ultra that began in 1974. Bradley, and the senior American commanders with access to Ultra, could not explain that the halt order was prompted by knowledge of the German plans, since this would clearly imply that the Allies were reading German signals traffic. Even the official US Army history of the campaign, published in 1961, erroneously stated that "American intelligence officers did not seem aware of Eberbach's mission to launch a massive attack against the deep XV Corps left flank." As a result, other explanations had to be offered. Many of these explanations were not particularly convincing, further fueling the controversy.

In his 1951 autobiography, Bradley suggested that the halt order was issued since the capture of Argentan had already been assigned to British/Canadian forces and a head-on meeting of US and Canadian forces would have been "a dangerous and uncontrollable maneuver." Bradley offered a second and more plausible rationale that he preferred "a solid shoulder at Argentan to a broken neck at Falaise." In retrospect, this vaguely hinted at his knowledge of the Panzergruppe Eberbach attack plan, without compromising the secret. The first details of the Ultra decrypts regarding Panzergruppe Eberbach were not public knowledge until 1988 with the publication of the relevant volume of Hinsley's history of British intelligence in World War II. By this time, dozens of sensationalistic books had been published, creating the Falaise controversy. The link between Panzergruppe Eberbach and the halt order has not been appreciated even in recent histories of the Normandy campaign.

ATTACK OR RETREAT?

Hitler continued to press Kluge and Eberbach to strike at XV Corps, even in the face of encirclement. In a directive received by Heeresgruppe B before dawn on Monday, August 14, Hitler castigated Kluge for the current situation: "The present situation in the rear of Heeresgruppe B is the result of the ill-planned and miscarried first attack on Avranches. Now that the enemy [XV Corps] has turned sharply west, there is a danger that Panzergruppe Eberbach, which was committed much too far north, will become bogged down in an inconclusive meeting engagement." Hitler went on to demand that II. SS-Panzer-Korps and the 21. Panzer-Division be added to Panzergruppe Eberbach's attack and he reiterated the need to attack the deep flank of XV Corps, not simply run into its forward combat elements.

In spite of Hitler's vociferous demands, Panzergruppe Eberbach could barely contain the Allied forces in the Argentan sector, never mind launch an attack. In conversations between Eberbach and Kluge on Monday, August 14, Eberbach reported that the roads around Argentan were clogged

An M4 medium tank fitted with a T2 Douglas hedgerow cutter, part of Task Force X, CCA, 3rd Armored Division, passes an abandoned 8.8cm Flak gun near Lougé-sur-Maire on August 17, 1944. The 3rd Armored Division fought a series of costly engagements with Panzergruppe Eberbach from the Rânes area on August 15 to Fromentel on August 17.

with retreating units, the Panzer divisions were too weak for offensive action, and the troops were increasingly demoralized by the continual air attacks. Eberbach had instructed his units to dig in and take up a defensive position. He urged Kluge to initiate a withdrawal out of the shrinking pocket while there was still time. At noon on Monday, August 14, the Canadian First Army launched Operation *Tractable* heading for Falaise. The situation in Normandy was reaching a crisis.

Tuesday, August 15 was later described by Hitler as "the worst day of my life." Canadian forces erupted out of the Caen sector and were heading toward Falaise against disintegrating German defenses. Patton's Third US Army was on a rampage with 7th Armored Division approaching Chartres and 4th Armored Division on the outskirts of Orléans, deep behind German lines. To add to Hitler's misery, the Seventh US Army conducted Operation *Dragoon*, the amphibious invasion of France's Mediterranean coast. Not only was Heeregruppe B in northern France under threat of annihilation, but so was Heeresgrupe G in central and southern France. German control of France was now in doubt.

Under these catastrophic circumstances, Kluge pushed Jodl to give him a "free hand" to extricate Heeresgruppe B from the Falaise–Argentan trap. Impatient, at 1440hrs Kluge issued his own withdrawal order. Hitler's permission finally arrived two hours later, but contained the demand that Panzergruppe Eberbach widen the exit by a Panzer strike to clear XV Corps away from Argentan. This was entirely hopeless and at 0200hrs on August 16, Kluge telephoned Jodl at OKW headquarters that the Panzer counter-attack was impossible due to a lack of fuel and ammunition. German troops began the retreat out of the Falaise pocket after sunset on Wednesday, August 16, 1944.

The German retreat from the Falaise pocket lasted nearly five days. The pocket was not closed until Monday, August 21 when troops of the Polish 1st Armored Division from II Canadian Corps linked up with elements of XV Corps near Chambois. The reasons for the delay in closing the Falaise pocket on August 15–18 remain controversial and are outside the scope of this short book.

A heavily camouflaged M10 3in. GMC of the 703rd Tank Destroyer Battalion during the fighting near Lougé-sur-Maire on August 17, 1944. Behind it to the left is a destroyed German half-track towing an 8.8cm Flak gun and to the right is a burned-out M4 medium tank of the 32nd Armored Regiment, 3rd Armored Division from Task Force X.

Hitler was extremely angry at the recent conduct of operations in Normandy, and on August 17, Kluge was sacked and replaced by Generalfeldmarschall Walter Model. Expecting to be arrested due to his knowledge of the July bomb plot, Kluge committed suicide on August 18. With the chances for an Argentan Panzer offensive no longer conceivable, Eberbach returned to the command of 5. Panzer-Armee. Panzergruppe Eberbach was never formally dissolved, but its component divisions gradually reverted to their original commands during the retreat through the Falaise–Argentan Gap. To complete the purge of officers suspected of involvement in the July bomb plot, Funck was relieved from command of 47. Panzer-Korps; Schwerin returned to command the 116. Panzer-Division.

IN RETROSPECT

The initial phase of Operation *Lüttich* failed for a variety of reasons. Heeresgruppe B was unable to mass a sufficiently large force to conduct the Avranches attack in the first few days of August 1944 since the Panzer units in 7. Armee were too battered by Operation *Cobra*. The Panzer divisions in 5. Panzer-Armee were too far away for immediate commitment and could not be extracted until infantry divisions replaced them. By the time that this substitution took place, Bradley's 12th Army Group had moved several divisions into the Avranches–Mortain area, making a Panzer penetration all the more problematic. As Hausser had warned, the *bocage* terrain in this area was unsuitable for mechanized operations. Allied intelligence successes and the Allied air power threw the balance further in the Allies favor. Not only was the first phase of Operation *Lüttich* launched too late, it was conducted in an intelligence vacuum with little appreciation by Berlin of the American order of battle around Mortain or the dubious fitness of the German divisions taking part in the attack. The decision to conduct

A column of GIs from the 80th Division enters Argentan on August 20, 1944. This city remained the center of resistance for Panzergruppe Eberbach in mid-August.

Operation *Lüttich* was symptomatic of Hitler's reflexive reliance on counter-attacks as the solution to battlefield challenges, even in circumstances that were far from ideal for such tactics.

Aside from failing in its mission to reach Avranches and restore the Normandy defense line, the first phase of Operation *Lüttich* also managed to upset the delicate balance of German forces in Normandy. The bulk of the Panzer forces, which had been concentrated along the Caen–Falaise axis in June and July, were now shifted further westward to deal with the expanding American threat. While this was an understandable response to the threats posed by Operation *Cobra*, it also moved the best of the German Normandy forces too far west, placing them deeper and deeper into the emerging encirclement trap. Hitler's insistence on reinvigorating Operation *Lüttich* using Panzergruppe Eberbach compounded this problem by shifting even more Panzer forces westward in spite of the growing threat of encirclement at Falaise–Argentan. Not only was Berlin ignorant about the strength of enemy forces, but it appears to have been largely unaware of the rapidly declining power of its own Normandy forces. Hitler grossly overestimated the combat potential of Panzergruppe Eberbach and there does not appear to have been even the most rudimentary attempt to assess its strength during the critical days after the start of Operation *Lüttich*. These misadventures drained the strength of the Panzer forces in Normandy and accelerated the encirclement of Heeregruppe B.

Although the heavy losses suffered in the fighting were the most obvious cause, the extended road marches combined with shortages of fuel and spares led to a steady attrition of the Panzer divisions during the week of August 7–15. The disjointed fighting around Alençon–Argentan probably led to the final crippling of Panzergruppe Eberbach. By the time that the final evacuation orders arrived on August 16, Panzergruppe Eberbach had already lost most of its combat power and was no longer in a position to substantially assist in keeping the Falaise–Argentan Gap open.

THE BATTLEFIELD TODAY

Like many of the battlefields in northern France away from the D-Day beaches, there are few major memorials to the fighting connected to Operation *Lüttich*, nor any commemorative museums. There is a small monument to the 30th Division on Hill 314, located a short distance from La Petite Chapelle on the southern side of the hill. The battlefield has not changed much since World War II, and a useful guide to the major sites is Robert Mueller's book listed below.

The memorial to the 30th Division on Hill 314 near Mortain. (© Alan Hughes / Wikimedia Commons / CC-BY-SA-3.0)

FURTHER READING

This book was prepared from primary and secondary sources. US Army records are located at the National Archives and Records Administration (NARA II) in College Park, Maryland. I used the records of the key US Army divisions in Records Group 407, including the after-action reports, S-3 journals, and combat interviews as well as similar records of other key separate battalions. There is an extensive selection of published accounts of Mortain, including divisional histories, and memoirs. The recent French study on the liberation of the Sarthe region by Fabrice Avoie is the best account of the fighting between XV Corps and the German opponents to the south and east of Mortain.

German records for Operation *Lüttich* are less extensive than in the American case due to the loss of many records in 1945. For example, there are few surviving records of 47. Panzer-Korps or the Panzer divisions for the 1944 time period. The Foreign Military Studies (FMS) program conducted in Germany after World War II attempted to collect the reminiscences of key German combat leaders, and I have listed some of the most relevant tiles of those that I used. The separate FMS "R" series were prepared by the staff of the US Army Center of Military History to support the preparation of the official US Army "Green Book" on the Normandy campaign by Martin Blumenson. These are based on captured German records and tend to focus on the higher command levels including the OKW, OB West, and 7. Armee. Copies are retained at NARA II. There is no major German study of Operation *Lüttich*, though the battle is covered in some of the divisional histories. The 116. Panzer-Division is especially well covered both by Deprun's detailed study as well as the memoirs of Heinz Guderian's son, who served in the unit during this period.

The Hinsley study is an excellent starting point for an examination of the impact of the Ultra signals intelligence program on this campaign. A large portion of messages sent to field commanders were microfilmed after the declassification program in the late 1970s and are available at a few major libraries. I used the microfilm collection prepared by Clearwater Publishing located at the Library of Congress in Washington DC.

UNPUBLISHED GOVERNMENT REPORTS AND DOCUMENTS

Adair, L., *et al.*, *Defensive, Deliberate Defense: 30th Infantry Division, 9–13 August 1944*, Command & General Staff School, Fort Leavenworth, 1983

Eberbach, Hans, *Panzer Group Eberbach and the Falaise Encirclement*, FMS A-922, 1946.

First United States Army, Report of Operations 1 August 1944–22 February 1945, 1946

Gersdorff, Rudolf Freiherr von, *Avranches Counter-attack, 7 Armee 29 Jul–14 Aug 1944*, FMS A-921

Gersdorff, Rudolf Freiherr von, *The Campaign in Northern France: The German Counter-attack against Avranches, Vol. IV, Chapter 4*, FMS B-725, 1946

Hausser, Paul, *Seventh Army, 20 Jun–20 Aug 1944*, FMS A-907, 1945

Hodgson, James, *German Troops in the Attack on Avranches, 3–7 August 1944*, FMS R-32, May 1953

Hodgson, James, *Breakout and Pursuit: Major Shifts of German Division on the Normandy Front 30 Jul–25 Aug 1944*, FMS R-33, 1955

Hodgson, James, *Thrust/Counter-Thrust: The Battle of France 21 Jul–25 Aug 1944*, FMS R-58, 1955

Jackson, William, *et al.*, *Employment of Four Tank Destroyer Battalions in the ETO*, Armored School, 1950

Jolasse, Erwin, *9 Panzer Division, 24 Jul–4 Sep 1944*, FMS B-837, 1946

Karamales, Lloyd, *et al.*, *Anti-Armor Defense Data Study, Volume II: US Anti-Tank defense at Mortain, France, August 1944*, Science Applications International Corp., 1990

Kerley, Ralph, *Operations of the 2nd Battalion, 120th Infantry (30th Infantry Division) at Mortain, France 6–12 August 1944: Personal Experience of a Company Commander*, Infantry School, Fort Benning, 1950

Lüttwitz, Heinrich von, *2nd Panzer Division, 6 Jun–24 Jul 1944*, FMS B-257, 1946

Lüttwitz, Heinrich von, *2nd Panzer Division, 26 Jul–6 Sep 1944*, FMS A-904, 1945

Lüttwitz, Heinrich von, *2nd Panzer Division, Attack on Alençon 13 Aug 1944*, FMS A-856, 1945

Müller, Gerhard, *116 Panzer Division, 11–24 Aug 1944*, FMS B-162, 1946

Richardson, James, *The Operations of the 1st Battalion, 39th Infantry (9th Division) at Chérénce-le-Roussel, France, 4–10 August 1944 during the German Attack on Avranches*, Infantry School, Fort Benning, 1948

Schmidt, Hans, *275 Infantry Division: Defensive Fighting at Mortain*, FMS B-370, 1948

Schwerin, Gerhard Graf von, *116 Panzer Division in Normandy*, FMS ETHINT-17, 1945

Schwedo, Bradford, *XIX Tactical Air Command and ULTRA: Patton's Force Enhancers in the 1944 Campaign in France*, Air University, Maxwell AFB, 2001

Thornblom, Carlton, *Operations of the 1st Battalion, 320th Infantry (35th Division) in the Attack on Mortain, France, 10–12 August 1944*, Infantry School, 1950

ULTRA: Main Series of Signals Conveying Intelligence to Allied Commands Based on Intercepted Radio Messages, Clearwater Publishing, NY: 1979–83. (Microfilm reels 34-36)

BOOKS

Avoie, Fabrice, *Histoire d'une Libération: Sarthe, août 1944*, Self-published: Le Mans, 2009

Blumenson, Martin, *Breakout and Pursuit*, Center of Military History: Washington DC, 1961

Bradley, Omar, *A Soldier's Story*, Henry Holt: New York, 1951

Buisson, Jules et Gilles, *Mortain et sa bataille: 2 août–13 août 1944*, Livre d'Histoire: Paris, 2004

Collins, J. Lawton, *Lightning Joe: An Autobiography*, Louisiana State University Press: Baton Rouge, 1979

Copp, Terry, (ed.) *Montgomery's Scientists: Operational Research in Northwest Europe*, Wilfred Laurier University: Ontario, 1999

Deprun, Frédéric, *Panzer en Normandie: Histoire des équipages de char de la 116. Panzerdivision Juillet–août 1944*, Ysec: Louviers, 2011

Dijke, Jacques van, *Entre le marteau et l'enclume: Von Kluge face à l'effrondement allemande juillet–août 1944*, Ysec, Louviers, 2009

Featherston, Allyn, *Saving the Breakout: The 30th Division's Heroic Stand at Mortain, August 7–12, 1944*, Presidio: Novato, 1993

Frappe, Jean-Bernard, *La Luftwaffe face au débarquement allié, 6 juin au 31 août 1944*, Heimdal: Bayeux, 1999

Gooderson, Ian, *Air Power at the Battlefront: Allied Close Air Support in Europe 1943–45*, Frank Cass: London, 1998.

Guderian, Heinz Günther, *From Normandy to the Ruhr with the 116th Panzer Division in World War II*, Aberjona: Bedford, PA, 2001

Hewitt, Robert, *Work Horse of the Western Front: The Story of the 30th Infantry Division*, Infantry Journal Press: Washington DC, 1946

Hinsley, F. H., *et al.*, *British Intelligence in the Second World War, Vol. 3, Part 2*, HMSO: London, 1988

Hogan, David, *A Command Post at War: First Army Headquarters in Europe 1943–45*, Center of Military History: Washington, DC, 2000

Knickerbocker, H. R., *et al.*, *Danger Forward: The Story of the First Division in World War II*, Battery Press: Nashville, 2002

Lehmann, Rudolf, and Tiemann, Ralf, *The Leibstandarte, Vol. IV/1*, Federowicz: Winnipeg, 1993

Mitcham, Samuel, *Panzer Commanders of the Western Front*, Stackpole: Mechanicsburg, 2008

Mueller, Robert, *Fields of War: The Battle of Normandy, Visitor's Guide to WWII Battlefields*, French Battlefields, Buffalo Grove: 2014

Reardon, Mark, *Victory at Mortain: Stopping Hitler's Panzer Counteroffensive*, University Press of Kansas: Lawrence, 2002

Shores, Christopher, and Thomas, Chris, *2nd Tactical Air Forcve, Vol. 2: Breakout to Bodenplatte July 1944 to January 1945*, Classic: Harsham, 2005

Spearhead in the West: The 3rd Armored Division 1941-1945, Battery Press: Nashville, 1980

The 35th Infantry Division in World War II, Battery Press: Nashville, 1988

Vannoy, Allyn, and Karamales, Jay, *Against the Panzers: United States Infantry versus German Tanks 1944–45*, McFarland: Jefferson, 1996

Weidinger, Otto, *2 SS Panzer Division Das Reich, Vol. V*, Federowicz: Winnipeg, 2012

Weiss, Robert, *Fire Mission: The Siege at Mortain, Normandy, August 1944*, White Main: Shippensburg, 2002.

Wind, M., and Günther, H. (eds.), *Kriegstagebuch 17.SS-Panzergrenadier-Division 30 Oktober 1943 bis 6 Mai 1945*, Schild: Munich, 1993

Wood, M., and Dugdale, J., *Orders of Battle: Waffen SS Panzer Units in Normandy 1944*, Books International, Farnborough, 2000

INDEX

Page numbers in **bold** refer to illustrations and their captions.